Wisdom
of the
Mystic Masters

Wisdom
of the
Mystic Masters

Joseph J. Weed

Parker Publishing Company, Inc.   West Nyack, New York

Reward Edition . . . . . May, 1973

This book is a reference work based on research by
the author. The opinions expressed herein are not
necessarily those of or endorsed by the Publisher.

Introduction

This book is written to help you achieve a fuller, better life. You have a right to happiness. I want to help you attain it. You may want and need a home and security, love or friendship, or perhaps money. These can all be yours if you first gain understanding, if you know what to do and how to do it.

The Rosicrucian Order, a non-profit teaching fraternity or brotherhood, devotes itself to teaching people like yourself and myself. Its training methods are thorough. The course is long and covers every phase of life as we know it. A person can spend many years studying it, as I have, and find something new and exciting in each lesson. But today few people have the time for years of introspective study. Life is moving at a more rapid pace and if one is to learn at all he or she must learn quickly—and now.

It is for this reason I have decided to condense into this book the knowledge and training methods I have acquired in thirty years of study.

The Rosicrucians have taught for many hundreds of years that we use only a very small fraction of our total ability. Brain specialists now confirm this. Dr. George Crile of Cleveland, an outstanding authority, has stated the average man normally uses less than 5 percent of his brain capacity and even the greatest geniuses rarely employ more than 15 percent. What a great race of beings we would be if we put to use just half of our physical equipment.

The Rosicrucians maintain that every man and woman can develop these innate abilities. More than this, they say that if you wish to take your place in the world as a responsible citizen you have an obligation to awaken the dormant areas of your being. Some years ago, John Dickson, then publisher of a great Chicago daily newspaper, expressed this need vividly when he said,

> Life is like a railroad. The vast majority of people are passenger coaches and freight cars. They perform a useful service but they cannot make themselves go and have to be pushed or pulled by someone else. Only a few are like the locomotives that move not only themselves but also countless others. Without them we would have no progress, humanity would stagnate and eventually drift into savagery.

The Rosicrucians say it lies within the capacity of everyone to be a "locomotive," and I propose to show you how you can become one. Now, for the first time in book form are given here the training methods of the Rosicrucians. When studied and practiced, these techniques will enable you to unfold your nature and exert control over yourself and your environment.

Let me make this clearer. There is a Rosicrucian I know, a widow, who lives on one of the islands of the West Indian Commonwealth. She is fond of solitude and her material wants are simple. So when her soldier husband was killed she bought a house and a few acres of land on this island. She has a small pension and rounds out her income by raising chickens, so all her needs are met.

Not long ago one of the great windstorms that come in August and September—hurricanes they are sometimes called—struck her island. When it had passed she found that her house, sturdily built and closely shuttered, was intact but that her chicken house was destroyed. This was a serious blow, because she did not have the money for a new one. So she bethought herself of her Rosicrucian teachings and resolved to put the principles to work.

The following morning it was necessary to check over the property and find out if any serious damage had resulted from the storm. Fortunately, only a few trees were down but in a small clearing about two hundred yards from her house was a great surprise. There, completely intact sat a fine, strong, new-looking chicken house. It had not been there before the storm, so she could only conclude that the great wind in its freakish way had deposited it there. She told everyone in the nearby village but when after a week no one had come to claim it, she had it moved into her chicken yard, where it stands to this day.

The mechanics of this are unimportant. It might just as well have happened in another way. She might have received an unexpected legacy, or someone might have come along with a desire to buy an unused piece of her property. But the fact remains that she needed and wanted a chicken house; she used her Rosicrucian knowledge and she got it. You, too, can perform the same kind of service for yourself when you understand the Rosicrucian teachings and have trained yourself in their techniques.

Much has been written and taught about the use of the mind. There are literally hundreds of books and treatises which tell you how to get rich or how to get well or how to win friends by using the mind. These are all quite true. The mind is a most powerful instrument. There is no doubt about it. But it is not easy for the average person like you or me to learn how to use the mind. We must learn something about ourselves first. We must understand our own human nature before we can really put our minds to work. It is access to this knowledge, this fully rounded understanding that I give to you in this book. Take it. Study it. Learn the truth about yourself and the world in which you live. Train yourself so that you may unfold your innate abilities and exert control over yourself and your environment.

If you would be a healer and bring healing strength to yourself and others study these chapters well. Everyone has the capacity to heal. Learn how to use this ability which is in you and give generously of your new-found strength that you and those near you may grow in health and well-being.

If you need more of the wealth of the material world, you are entitled to it. There are two whole chapters which will help you find the solution to this problem—and help you find peace of mind as well.

If you are interested in telepathy, you can train yourself to be sensitive to others' thoughts and feelings and in turn impress them with your own.

If you happen to be concerned about death—and many people

are—study the Chapter on Birth, Death and Reincarnation. The body may weaken and disintegrate and you may have to leave it but your conscious awareness of yourself and your surroundings continues without interruption. When you have had just one successful experience with etheric projection as described and taught in Chapter Thirteen and for the first time found yourself out of your body and in full possession of all your faculties, you will never fear death again. Once you succeed in this practice, the greatest and most sublime experiences await you.

Take this book. Keep it near you always. Refer to it in need. Let it help you in every way. That in it you may find the path to a richer, healthier and more rewarding life is my most earnest wish for you.

Contents

THE ROSICRUCIANS ARE PROBABLY BEST KNOWN FOR THEIR REMARKABLE ACCOMPLISHMENTS IN HEALING. EVEN RELATIVE NEWCOMERS TO THE TEACHING FREQUENTLY ACHIEVE SURPRISING CURES. HEALING IS SO IMPORTANT AN ENTIRE CHAPTER IS DEVOTED TO IT. IN THE PRESENT CHAPTER THE HUMAN BODY AS ROSICRUCIANS UNDERSTAND IT AND THE IMPORTANCE OF BALANCE IN KEEPING IT WELL IS EXPLAINED. THIS BALANCE IS REFERRED TO AS "HARMONIUM." ONCE YOU UNDERSTAND HARMONIUM AND HOW TO MAINTAIN IT, YOU NEED NEVER BE SICK AGAIN.

WE SAY "ALL MEN ARE CREATED EQUAL" BUT WE MEAN BY THIS "ALL MEN ARE ENTITLED TO EQUAL OPPORTUNITY AND HAVE EQUAL RIGHTS BEFORE GOD." NO ONE IS SO BLIND OR FOOLISH AS TO IMAGINE THERE IS ACTUAL EQUALITY OF ABILITY OR ENVIRONMENT OR PHYSICAL EQUIPMENT OR CONDITIONS OF BIRTH BETWEEN MEN. THESE INEQUITIES EXIST BUT THEY CAN BE OVERCOME. THIS CHAPTER TELLS WHY THEY EXIST AND BY UNDERSTANDING THEM HOW YOU CAN MAKE OR REMAKE YOUR FUTURE.

WHAT HAPPENS AFTER DEATH? FACTUAL REPORTS, NOT ROMANTIC IMAGINING. THE DEVELOPMENT OF CONSCIOUSNESS IN THE INDIVIDUAL IS LARGELY RESPONSIBLE FOR AFTERLIFE EXPERIENCES. DESCRIPTION OF VARIOUS LEVELS OF EXPERIENCE AND REASONS FOR THIS. HOW DEVELOPMENT MAY CONTINUE BETWEEN INCARNATIONS. REBIRTH. WHAT TAKES

PLACE BEFORE BIRTH AND WHY. APPROACHES TO THE NEW LIFE. EX-
AMPLES. QUOTATIONS FROM ROSICRUCIAN EXPERIENCES.

TO DEVELOP THEM. MANTRAMS. VISUALIZATIONS. COLOR. THOUGHT. RE-
SULTS TO BE EXPECTED. CLAIRAUDIENCE. CLAIRVOYANCE. INSPIRATION.
INTUITION. ILLUMINATION. CONTACT WITH A HIGHER BEING.

HOW TO BE IN TWO PLACES AT ONCE. ETHERIC PROJECTION. ASTRAL PRO-
JECTION. MENTAL PROJECTION. TECHNIQUES FOR MASTERING EACH ART
WITH PRACTICAL EXERCISES. HOW TO APPEAR TO OTHERS AND HAVE THEM
RECOGNIZE YOU. EXAMPLES. CASE HISTORIES.

THE PURPOSE OF THE ROSICRUCIAN ORDER, ITS AGE AND TRADITIONAL
ORIGIN. FAMOUS ROSICRUCIANS. HOW KNOWLEDGE IS DISSEMINATED BY
ROSICRUCIANS IN ADVANCE OF "SCIENTIFIC DISCOVERY."

Wisdom
of the
Mystic Masters

ONE

The Human Body:
How to Understand Yourself
and Attain Harmonium

In the Golden Age of Greece at the time of the great philosophers the words "Gnothe Seauton" were inscribed in large letters over the entrance to the Athenian Temple. This means "Know Thyself," which was considered the primary essential to all knowledge by the wise men of that time. So in this first chapter I want to help you to get to know yourself better so that you will find it easier to understand and work with the instructions given later on in the book.

You probably think that you already know yourself very well. From one point of view you may. You have within you a record of all you have done and all that has happened to you since you were born. If you can translate all of this action into true understanding you do not need this book. But the chances are ten thousand to one that you cannot, and do not. For example, if you have a headache, what do you do? Most people take a headache remedy and try to get relief from the pain as quickly as possible. Then, when comfortable at last, they give it no further thought. Very few try to seek out the cause. Sometimes, of course, the cause is all too obvious. Yet even then the tendency is to seek relief of the effect, the headache, rather than correct the cause.

Having spent your entire life with this body of yours, you should now know it better than this. Headaches are not necessary. And even when sudden, unexpected pressures do create one, you should know how to eliminate it quickly and easily without pills or other medication. If you cannot, you do not know much about yourself.

You have tremendous capacities, far more and far greater than you suspect. You have been taught, or you have taught yourself, certain skills of hand or mind in order that you may contribute the fruits of these skills to the general economy and thus earn a livelihood. This is normal practice. Yet if you had been encouraged to spend the same time and effort in learning about yourself and proper instruction had been available to you your contribution to the general good would be ten, twenty or fifty times greater than it is and the rewards to you proportionate. Since it is never too late to learn, start now to study yourself.

The Rosicrucians teach that we have a dual nature, a material body occupied and energized by a spiritual essence. This is not a new idea by any means. It is basic to all major religions, most of which call the internal essence the "soul." In recent years science has begun to adopt a similar view. Many men prominent in the fields of biology and biological chemistry now admit to the existence of an intangible something which affects the material being, a "something" which they are not yet prepared to identify. This seems very much like the soul of the religionists.

The Rosicrucians say every human being uses two kinds of energy, physical energy and soul (or physic) energy. Our physical energy comes to us from what we eat and drink and from the air we breathe. A small part of our psychic energy comes to us this way but most of it comes through our psychic centers. These centers can be likened to transformers which tap the sea of energy around us and condition it for our use.

One Great Sea of Vibrating Energy

Now here is a new idea, you say. What is this about a "sea of energy"? The Rosicrucians teach that all is energy vibrating at different rates. Everything we can see, feel, smell, hear or taste is a form of vibrating energy. A hundred years ago this idea was very difficult for people to accept but today we know, and all of our scientists agree, that physical matter is made up of atoms which in turn are composed of electrons and protons and neutrons all in violent motion, in other words particles of energy moving at incredibly high speeds. The Rosicrucians go a step further and maintain that not only the material world which we see, but the air we breathe and the space beyond from here to the stars is one great sea of vibrating energy.

The physical world vibrates at a relatively slow rate but as you move away from it to higher levels, the vibratory rate increases while the texture becomes finer and more tenuous. This finer energy is not only out in space but all around us. In it "we live, move and have our being." This is the energy which our psychic centers pick up and transform (step down) for our use in physical, emotional and mental action. We will study vibrations and the psychic centers in detail later on but for the present all we need know is that they function in everyone and in some more efficiently than in others.

When this psychic energy is stepped down to a point where it is used by the physical body, it manifests itself very much like electrical energy, only more subtly. Like electricity, it has polarity and this polarity can be controlled. Most people have too much energy of negative polarity and not enough positive. Thus they are out of balance. Balance is very difficult to achieve and even more difficult to maintain. The Rosicrucians call perfect balance "harmonium." In the chapter on healing, this is discussed in detail. Too much food and all low-grade emotions tend to overbalance your body to the negative side. When you become too "negative" some sort of illness is manifested. This is your body's way of telling you that you have been doing something wrong and to stop it. It is also possible to overbalance yourself on the positive side and this usually results in nervous tensions or mental illness. It is well to remember that the ideal is a state of equilibrium and to strive to achieve this. A completely practical method is to be moderate in all you eat and drink, to refrain from indulging the lower emotions and to think clearly—and often. This latter is not a joke. None of us thinks enough, really thinks.

Usually when we imagine we are thinking we are merely playing or replaying an old emotional record in our minds.

Attaining Harmonium

Many normal everyday things have an elevating influence on us and help us approach the much desired harmonium. The contemplation of beauty in any of its forms is helpful. Laughter, too, is a great healer. And, of course, clear thought. But in addition the Rosicrucians offer exercises which are designed to create the necessary counterbalance in order to bring you nearer harmonium. These are now explained.

One exercise is designed to correct a condition which is excessively negative and the other is designed to accomplish the opposite objective, namely to correct an over-positive condition. In using these exercises, select a spot where you will not be disturbed for about ten minutes. Sit in a straight-backed chair. Take three deep easy breaths to relax yourself and then proceed with the proper exercise.

To Counterbalance a Negative Condition

Separate your feet but keep them placed squarely on the floor. Sit erect and allow your hands to lie loosely in your lap or on your knees without touching each other. The index and middle finger and the thumb of each hand must be held touching each other in a sort of triangle composed of the first two fingers and thumb. When you are finally relaxed, take a deep breath, hold it for a count of seven and then release it easily. After a short rest, repeat this, taking another deep breath and holding it for the count of seven. Then rest and repeat this until you have done it seven times, after which change your position and put the whole procedure out of your mind.

This exercise is normally adequate to counterbalance the average negative condition. However, in cases of deep-seated or chronic ailments it will need repeating. Always wait at least two hours between treatments because it usually takes that long for results to become apparent. The earlier you treat yourself when falling out of balance, the easier it is to come back to normal. So be aware of yourself and when you feel the least bit out of sorts give yourself a treatment to regain your positive-negative balance.

To Counterbalance an Over-Positive Condition

Sit comfortably as in the previous treatment. This time your feet should be touching each other, squarely on the floor but touching. Your hands must also be touching at the fingers. Hold them in front of your body at the chest level, thumb touching thumb and each finger touching the tip of its corresponding finger on the other hand. Now close your eyes and take a deep breath. Exhale slowly and when the air is all out of your lungs, hold it out for the count of five. Then breathe in and out easily and slowly for about five or six breaths until you are once again relaxed. Then repeat, holding the breath out for the count of five. Repeat the entire procedure five times, then stop, breathe normally and put the entire exercise out of mind.

This so-called negative treatment (to counterbalance excess positive) is exceptionally effective in treating the common cold if practiced in the early stages of infection. The cold symptoms are the outward evidence of your system's attempt to rid itself of an invasion by certain types of hostile microorganisms. A "positive" treatment does no good in these situations but the "negative" treatment described here will usually aid the system to defeat and cast out (or subdue) the hostile germs in about six to eight hours. Three such treatments an hour or two apart should be adequate.

The wonderful part of these treatments is that if you err and use the positive where the negative is called for, or vice versa, there are no harmful effects. They are physical counterbalances which aid mechanically in bringing the system back into proper balance, so if the wrong treatment is used it does not aggravate the imbalanced condition. Study yourself and observe results. Soon you will be aware of the slightest physical disturbance.

Trial and error will enable you to determine which treatment is best in each case. When in doubt, both can be used. Quick action on your part will help you keep in constant balance, which will evidence itself in robust good health.

It is very difficult for us to see ourselves as we really are. We have been conditioned from earliest childhood to ignore all but the most vigorous and solid impacts upon our consciousness. We are trained by life and by our elders to be materialists Small wonder, therefore, we give so little value to the spiritual and attach so much importance to the physical and its correlative emotions. Since that is true for all of us, it is foolhardy to ignore the physical or, worse still, try to pretend it does not exist. Far better, give it full recognition and use it as the foundation upon which a higher awareness is built. This deliberate expansion of consciousness is a step-by-step progression along a path for which this book serves as a guide.

From the very beginning you must learn to be more aware, not less so. Most young people are vitally alive. Every impact upon their consciousness, whether it be physical, emotional or mental, is a vivid experience. But as they grow older, the sharp edge is dulled and many become only half alive. It is important for you to attain and hold a youthful attitude toward your everyday experiences. Each impact upon your senses must be given full attention, savored so to speak. At first this will require extra effort but before long it will become habitual and therefore easy. At this point in your training you must begin to ask yourself "why?" Why did I feel good when I heard a certain remark? What is there in my make-up which caused this sudden surge of pleasure within me? Or conversely, why was I so cast down when this man, a relative stranger to me, failed to return my greeting? What are the mechanics of this inside of me? Why should I be affected one way or the other?

Or going a step further, ask, What was it I said or did that caused two former friends to suddenly become antagonistic? It is important to seek in one's self for causes and not blame others. The most successful people are always keenly aware of their impact upon others. Are you? Or do you just react to words and events without question?

First Step into a Higher Awareness

This is the way one begins a study of one's self. It is not difficult. It requires only that you give it your attention and interest. But simple though it seems, it is the first step into a higher awareness, a step from the world of effects into the world of causes. As you progress you will see that certain of your words and actions are unworthy of the image you have of yourself and you will correct them. As you do this, you will in time come to realize you have adopted a higher standard and that many of your former worries, frustrations and defeats no longer trouble you. True, events in your life may not have changed to any noticeable degree, but you will now see them in a new perspective, one in which you are no longer a pawn of fate but a powerful individual who is beginning to have a hand in the creation of his destiny.

The Rosicrucians teach that knowledge is power. As you gain a greater insight into the way things really are and acquire a knowledge of causes, you will find the ability to generate certain causes and control their effects. This is power. In achieving it you must go carefully. Remember that the world in which you live is a gigantic laboratory with people like chemicals all interacting with each other and affecting the whole. Each act of yours, everything you do, or say, or think, yes, even every emotion you give way to, has an impact on everyone else. You can attain the rank of master chemist in this laboratory if you but follow diligently the instructions given.

Many people believe Rosicrucianism to be a religion. This is not so. The Rosicrucians have no dogma, an essential in every world religion. They do not require that you believe anything they teach. You may accept or not, as you see fit. In fact the Rosicrucians seriously urge you not to accept anything that you cannot prove or in some other way satisfy yourself of its truth. Their teachings and writings are not based upon the statements of great spiritual leaders but are the accumulated discoveries and deductions of many men gathered over the course of centuries. Intelligent men, dedicated experimenters driven by the desire to know, are constantly improving and adding to the Rosicrucian teachings, and thus they are always a step ahead of accepted scientific thought. For example, the possibility of atomic power was suggested in monographs released in 1926 and some hints on its use were given. Another fact, equally true but not yet scientifically accepted, is that the warmth of this planet is not nearly so dependent upon the sun's rays as it is on the presence of meteoric dust in and around our upper atmosphere.

Thus, if what you read in this book seems reasonable, if you can prove it out by experiment or in some other way, accept it. But do not believe it because the Rosicrucians say so, or because I say so, or because anyone else says so. One of the big problems today is that so many people accept as true things that are not true at all, things that they believe because they regard them as coming from unimpeachable authority or simply because the people they know believe them and they have never encountered challenging ideas to the contrary. In this believing world Rosicrucians are often referred to as skeptics because we always seek proof and we always ask "why?"

So this book deals in facts and offers instruction only in those skills and abilities that have been successfully demonstrated by men and women like yourself.

TWO

The Principle of Karma: How You Can Make and Remake Your Future

The next step in gaining understanding of yourself and ultimate control of your destiny is a knowledge of karma. Karma is a Hindu word which literally means "action." Today its meaning is extended to refer to the results of action.

Many people understand karma as the working of the Law of Cause and Effect. This it is, true enough, but the definition is too broad. The Law of Cause and Effect applies on all planes and under all circumstances. A tumbling pebble on a mountainside can precipitate a landslide but it is only by a stretch of the imagination that we would refer to the landslide as a karmic result of the pebble in motion.

When we use the word karma we refer to results engendered by volitional action. Karma in its very essence implies the presence of motive, which in turn necessitates the exercise of free choice. More accurately, then, we may define karma as "the working of the Law of Cause and Effect as it applies to the results of decisions reached and thoughts held by ensouled forms capable of free choice." You are just such an ensouled form, as are all men, and it is karma as it applies to you that I will describe. However, you must not overlook the fact that groups of men, both small and large, permanent and temporary, are also ensouled forms and as such create karma. This accounts for group karma, which adheres to permanent groups such as the family,

9

city, nation and race, and also to temporary groups like societies, business organizations, corporations, clubs, etc.

In considering karma as it applies to you we will study:
1. Its causes.
2. Its working out or effects.
3. How it may be molded.
4. The steps to take to be liberated from it.

We are fond of saying "All men are created equal" but we ourselves do not accept this literally. No one is so blind, or so foolish as to imagine that there is actual equality of ability, or environment, or conditions of birth for all. Two questions arise, (1) Is this inequity the result of karma? and (2) Is it fair? The answer to both is "yes." You are today the end product of your own decisions and actions both recent and in the distant past. Every thought, every emotion or wish and every action creates karma and you as a thinking entity have been thus creating karma for thousands and possibly millions of years. If these thoughts, ideas, desires, passions and acts are benevolent, so-called good karma results. If they are malevolent, evil or difficult karma is created. Thus the good or evil we generate attaches itself to us and remains in our life current until we have satisfied it by balancing it out.

The laws of nature are invariable and immutable. Man recognizes this although he frequently attempts to defy these laws. The chemist in his laboratory knows he may expect certain well-defined results if he places two elements in close proximity in a definite set of conditions. If these results are not achieved he does not assume the law has changed but considers that he, himself, has made an error. Nature intends you to be happy and successful and to enjoy the fruits she so bountifully supplies. If this is not true for you, you may be sure you have broken natural law, either currently or in the past, and that you are now suffering the penalty for this infraction. This is not punishment in the sense that we punish evil-doers but rather a balancing out of energies. If you obey the law you may confidently predict a harmonious and happy result, for nature is conquered by obedience to her laws.

Karma Energized by Your Will

The most persistent and lasting karma comes from the thought forms that have been energized by your will. The great oriental Teacher, K. H., has described this as follows:

Every thought of man upon being evolved passes into the inner world and becomes an active entity by associating itself, coalescing we might term it, with an elemental—that is to say with one of the semi-intelligent forces of the more subtle kingdoms of matter. It survives as an active intelligence—a creature of the mind's begetting—for a longer or shorter period proportionate with the original intensity of the cerebral action which generated it. Thus a good thought is perpetuated as an active, beneficent power, an evil one as a maleficent demon. And so man is continually peopling his current in space with a world of his own, crowded with the offspring of his fancies, desires, impulses and passions, a current which reacts upon any sensitive or nervous organization which comes in contact with it in proportion to its dynamic intensity.

Now let us see what this means. In the average man's present stage of development every single one of his thoughts passes through and is colored by his desire body on the way to and from his active consciousness. Created originally as a mental entity, it comes into being as a vibrating force on the mental plane. These vibrations from the original idea or pattern which remain on the mental plane attract and mold the forces of each plane below the mental on its way to the active physical consciousness. The energetic creations so molded by the idea attach themselves to him and remain with him for a longer or shorter time, depending upon the original intensity of the thought which created them and, of course, the re-energizing effect that a repetition of this thought has upon them.

It is this cloud of self-created, energetic beings, elementals so to speak, existing in the finer grades of matter and hovering about you, that creates your karma. These active entities are responsible for what you know as sensation. They translate the vibrations that impinge upon your awareness into what is known and recognized by you as sight, feeling, taste, smell and sound. They manifest themselves physically in this manner and also more subtly, but very strongly, in the emotional field. Thus it is said that men live in a world of illusion peopled by the phantasms of their own creation.

The Cloud of Entities Around You

By your will, emotions and desires you are constantly influencing this cloud of entities around you and they sensitively respond to all the thrills of feeling that you send out. In just the same manner, but to a lesser degree, do these elementals respond to vibrations approaching them from without. This is the actual process of how you become aware of physical objects and it indicates how you can become aware of the feelings and thoughts of another.

Not only do you generate and send out thought forms but you act as a magnet to draw to you the thought forms of others. You may thus attract to yourself reinforcements of energy and it lies with you to decide whether these forces drawn from without shall be for good or evil. If your thoughts are pure and noble, you will attract hosts of beneficent entities. Sometimes you may wonder at the tremendous power of achievement which seems so far beyond normal ability that may come in answer to noble and unselfish effort. Every day the newspapers carry some such story— how a ninety-pound mother lifted the wheel of an automobile to free her small son caught beneath it; how a wounded marine in Vietnam carried his more seriously injured comrade through two miles of jungle swamps to get medical aid; how a 14-year-old girl swam four miles through rough water to the Florida shore to get help for her grandfather and small brother who were being carried along in the Gulfstream in an open boat with a damaged motor. The seeming impossible is accomplished when determination is accompanied by high purpose. This also is what Tennyson referred to when he wrote of Sir Galahad: "His strength was as the strength of ten because his heart was pure."

Conversely, low thoughts have a disturbing and evil effect, sometimes astonishingly beyond the actual intention of the individual. "Some devil must have tempted me," is the cry that is often heard, and it is true that these additional evil forces, sympathetic to and adding to his own wrong intentions, have provided the strength for the deed. Please observe—we are not "attacked" by these entities; we attract them to us.

At this point you may rightly question, "What is the difference between good and evil action and how may I distinguish it?" The answer I am sure you already know. A good thought, wish or act is one which conforms to the law of nature; evil is that which is at variance with nature's law. As to how to know the law—this requires the application of intelligence and good judgment. In the ultimate you will only know the law, really know it, through your own experience. However, you can learn it much more quickly and save yourself grief if you will accept and act on advice from more advanced souls who have already traveled along the road through life and encountered the same problems that beset you. These Elder Brothers, the Saints of the various churches, the Masters of Wisdom, have from time immemorial been precipitating into the consciousness of mankind advice and direction based upon their own experience. Thus, the words of Christ, "Love One Another," are not an abstract religious precept but a scientific technique found workable and successful by Him, which He has passed on to us as a shortcut to the working out and elimination of karma.

No Obstacle Too Great, No Problem Insoluble

The good thoughts or evil thoughts, desires and intentions which you create and harbor not only have an effect upon yourself but also often affect others. These elementals which you have endowed with your energy and which hover about you have a tendency to be attracted toward others of a similar kind. When you send out a thought form, it not only keeps a magnetic link with yourself but it is drawn toward other thought forms of a similar type These together accumulate to form a good or an

evil force, as the case may be, and to this aggregation of similar
thought forms are due the characteristics, often strongly marked,
of family or of local or national influence. This is very clear
today when a divergence between national ideologies is so well
defined, and you may also note that family or national karmic
surroundings largely modify the individual's activity and limit
to a very great extent his power to express the abilities he may
possess. Each idea is colored and distorted by the atmosphere
which surrounds him (and you) and its limitations are sometimes
far-reaching.

When this is realized, certain fainthearted ones throw up their
hands and say, "How can I ever overcome such weighty obstacles?"
This is the worst sin. No obstacle is too great to be overcome, no
problem is insoluble. Karmic difficulties are to teach and train,
not to punish. A Rosicrucian family had a small daughter born
with cerebral palsy. At the age of three she was lovely-looking
but still like a vegetable—no speech, no evidence of understanding, no control of physical movements. The parents were advised
to put her into an institution where she would be cared for and
no longer be the particular burden a child like that is in a large
and growing family. But the mother refused to do this and took
upon herself the herculean task of teaching this small girl how
to understand and to express herself in speech, how gradually
to control her body movements, all the thousand and one things
we take for granted but which in this case had to be painstakingly
taught. And all the while she brought up her other children and
did all the chores involved in running a home on a modest
income.

This was a karmic problem, unquestionably, and many years
later this mother had this confirmed. The daughter had been her
younger sister in another life. In a fit of jealousy she had pushed
her over a cliff and, though she survived, her body was broken
and she never walked again. In this life, the little girl grew to be
a beautiful, intelligent and charming woman, but yet she does
not walk, her only remaining weakness. Her mother could have
shirked a karmic responsibility and put her three-year-old daughter into an institution for the mentally retarded, for so she seemed
at the time. But she did not and her efforts have been rewarded

by a most beautiful achievement. The witty and charming young woman of today is a far cry from the little vegetable of twenty years ago. This alone is reward in itself. But the mother has had other rewards, not the least of which is the knowledge that she has paid a heavy debt and brought an old score into balance.

The Imperishable Film of the Akasha

So it is seen how a most difficult karmic problem was resolved and that the rewards were then out of proportion to the effort expended. This is also an example of how some karma is carried over to another life. Every thought, every wish, every desire and every act of ours is recorded in the imperishable film of the Akasha. There they remain and print out duplicates in the emotional and physical world life after life until satisfied or corrected. These desires and acts may be only noble and good, or they may be all evil, or they may be a combination of both. But even if they are all good and noble, there is still a karmic result and a karmic debt to be paid (or received) as long as the individual retains a self-conscious focus. But more of this later.

In considering the effect of karma or the working out of karma, I will concentrate only on its working in the physical life. It is quite true that karma has a great effect during the after life, the life between incarnations, but that is a deep study and not essential to our present observations. In the working of karmic law, we see that:

a. Aspirations and desires become abilities
b. Repeated thoughts become tendencies
c. Will to performance becomes action
d. Painful experiences become conscience
e. Repeated experiences lead to wisdom

The negative aspects of the foregoing produce negative results. For instance, the refusal to accept opportunity returns later in frustration, evil thoughts become evil tendencies and evil action results in a limiting of action such as a dwarfed mind, a diseased or mutilated body, a sudden and violent death, and so on.

In the working out of karma you will, if you are observant, see many strange things. You may find yourself in contact and close association with individuals who have been close to you before. Frequently these associations are repeated in many lives and they continue to appear and reappear until the energy given and taken comes into balance. Thus the tyrannical father of one life may reappear at a later time as a poor relative dependent for his very existence upon the whims of his former son. The loving and devoted mother may show herself in the future as a happy and well-cared-for sister, daughter or wife. We likewise owe debts to certain countries and for this reason may reappear again and again in the same land until we have discharged the obligation. We are led back there by those very tendencies and affinities which continue to attract us until balance is achieved and the accounts are written off the books.

It may seem that we have been placing a great deal of emphasis upon past lives and not enough on the present life. This is because not enough recognition is given to these more remote causes of our present conditions of life. Actually most of what you are today and what occurs to you stems from what you did last week or last year. But this you know and can easily take into account.

Conscience as the Beginning of Wisdom

Very gradually at first, but later with increasing speed, you learn from many repetitions and sometimes disastrous results that certain actions are against the law and must be avoided. There is built into your consciousness a recollection that wanton killing, for example, brings extremely unpleasant results for you. There comes a time when, faced with the temptation to kill, you are stricken in advance by a feeling which can only be described as a sort of remorse, a remorse for something you have not yet done. The temptation to kill is overcome by this remorseful feeling and you obey the law instead of breaking it. This peculiar feeling, this inner guidance, is known as conscience and it indicates the beginning of wisdom. If you are willing to listen to the voice of conscience every time you are faced with the necessity for a new and unique action, you will gradually come to know you have in it a never failing guidance which with use will become increasingly more and more successful in keeping you within the law.

It is at this point you begin to liquidate more debts than you currently contract, you begin to free yourself from some of the myriad of subtle beings that hover about you. You are learning the proper conduct in order that new karmic problems be avoided. You learn not to regret loss and not to be overjoyed at gain. You learn to live more for the sake of others and not so much for your own self-satisfaction. You learn to think not as an individual but as part of a group.

The law of karma may be likened to the physical law of momentum. A plate falls from a table. If allowed to strike the floor it will break. The result in a small way will be cataclysmic. But if the observer is quick, if he sees in advance what will happen and acts to prevent it, he can interpose his hands between the falling plate and the floor and either catch the plate or deflect it in such a way that the fall will be broken. The momentum generated by the falling body has either been met and opposed by an equal force or diverted by a force coming at an angle with the result that the impending damage does not occur.

It is in just such a manner that impending karmic results can be altered. As the student advances in knowledge and understanding, it is given to him to see certain karmic conditions which are about to precipitate themselves into action. To quote a modern example, he may learn that his home is situated on the San Andreas fault and therefore quite likely to suffer earthquake damage; so he counteracts this by the simple expedient of selling the house and moving away. Or again, he may meet a man, drawn together by karmic ties from the past, and observing that this man intends nothing but evil for him, he can refuse to contend with him. To fight back will only continue the warfare. The successful technique is to meet ill with good will, hate with love and so disarm and disintegrate the malevolent intentions of the other. It is in this simple manner that you may avert the worst blows of personal karma.

Therefore, send out truth against falsehood. Against selfishness oppose charity; in the presence of foulness, emanate purity. These actions, fiery in their essence, burn up the demons which karma may bring to your door.

It is true there may be no direct interference with karma, but you may modify its action by knowledge. When you understand this, you may use karmic force to effect karmic results and once more conquer nature by obedience to her laws.

Diverting Adverse Karmic Results

As knowledge grows you will find it easier and easier to rid yourself of the karma of the past. It will become possible to look backward and trace karmic lines right up to the present, so that action can be taken to counteract or divert the undesired karmic results. It will also become possible to look forward and see the effects in the future being generated by the actions of today. With such knowledge of causes you will be able to utilize the law and, relying on its unchangeability, set up effects in the future which you desire. In physics it is possible to neutralize a sound wave by setting up another sound wave of the same pattern which starts from the opposite pole. The result is equilibrium or silence. In just this same manner you can neutralize the vibrations of hatred, for example, by sending out against them the vibrations of love and reach thereby a much-desired equilibrium.

Karma can also be altered by thought, by a change in your outlook or mental attitude. The success of certain voodoo practices depends upon this factor, wherein the sick are made well or the healthy made sick by the suggestion of the obeah, or witch doctor. You may say that this is largely the result of suggestion and it cannot be disputed that the subconscious is the controlling factor, but the future for that individual does become different.

There is no question but that a decisive act can have a great bearing on your future. You can jump from the top of the Empire State building and conclusively end your future on the spot. Or you can decide to stop worrying about trifles and lengthen your life by ten years. There have been many stories written around the concept that the future is in some respects pre-ordained. In one story that I recall, the hero has three paths before him. Each path takes him to a different part of the world where the events that befall him are unique and unlike the events of either of the other paths. But in the end, on a certain day which is the same for all three, he is killed by a falling tree.

This concept may be true in some cases but it is certainly not true in all. Some people have two, three or four different possible dates on which their life may terminate and these are subject to the decisions and actions of the individual. The son of a New York Rosicrucian is a case in point. When he was quite young his mother was informed by her Teacher that the boy had two possible death points 15 years apart. The earlier date with fate was on European soil. Since he was living in New York, little thought was given to it. However, when he was twenty-one the United States got into World War II; he went to an officers' training school and within eight months' time was shipped to France. There, two days before his twenty-second birthday, as had been foretold, he was hit by a sniper's bullet and instantly killed. So you see that the time of death can sometimes depend upon where you are.

Your mental outlook—the way you see yourself and the world around you—has a very powerful influence upon your future. By changing your outlook you can change your future. Sometimes this can be done by using a device, or a so-called gimmick. Ed Wynn, the comedian, when he was 70 years old and no longer in demand as a performer, used a gimmick to effect a change in his future. It was something only he would think of. Half serious and half in jest he changed his birthday to a day fifteen years and four months later than the actual date. Instead of seventy years, he then only admitted to fifty-five, celebrated his birthday on the new day and in every way acted and gave the impression that the new date was correct.

Amazingly, his whole outlook changed. He felt younger and acted younger. Ideas for comedy acts came to him and before long he was working in a new television show and earning more money than ever before. Wynn, of course, was the one most affected by this artifice. He succeeded in convincing himself he was that much younger and acted accordingly. No one else was deceived. But the effect on Ed Wynn was so pronounced that he changed himself from a has-been to a star within a few months. In just such a manner can a change in mental attitude alter your future.

As long as any karmic ties remain we all shall, of necessity, return to the physical body again and again. Good karma drags us back as relentlessly as bad and the chain forged out of our virtues holds us just as firmly as that created by our vices. We shall only become free when we have learned the proper technique and this lies not in our actions but in our desires—or rather in our lack of desires. As long as there is the slightest tinge of self in any of our actions, as long as we are good because we hope for reward, then we shall have to return here in order to receive that reward. Every cause has its effect, every action its fruit, and desire is the cord that links them. When this thread is broken and burned out, the connection will end and the soul will be free. True, you will continue to live and act, but no longer for the self. Thought of self will then be gone and consciousness will gradually merge into the Larger Life.

THREE

Birth, Death and Reincarnation

So far I have given you very few training techniques, the exercises which are designed to develop your latent abilities. It is essential that you first understand yourself a little better and get to know more about the world in which you live. A great deal of what all of us are taught from childhood and what we grow up accepting as gospel is but a romanticized version of the actual facts. This is what Paul referred to when he wrote, "We see but through a glass, darkly." He understood this quite well because his own realization came very suddenly and he could still remember clearly what things had seemed like before that day on the road to Damascus. For most of us this awakening is so gradual we are scarcely aware of it and only come to realize what has taken place within us when we compare our present-day knowledge and understanding with that of several years ago.

The material in the first two chapters and in this, the third chapter, is greatly condensed from the Rosicrucian lessons given at intervals of a week over a period of nearly three years. The Rosicrucians believe, and wisely, that it is extremely difficult for most people to surrender the myths and misconceptions they acquired while growing up and so they go very slowly about the process of re-educating them. The size and scope of this book does not permit such deliberateness, so after the explanations on Birth and Death in this chapter I will plunge on into the course of training and hope you will have absorbed sufficient background to profit by it.

Have You Lived Other Lives? Will You Live Again?

The two greatest mysteries of life are birth, its beginning, and death, its ending. A great deal is known of the physical facts of both, but beyond the outward and obvious our most learned scientists and medical men know very little. There seems to be a superstitious prejudice against studying anything but the physical manifestations of life. Yet there is much to be learned by anyone who approaches these aspects of life with an open mind. There are so many unanswered questions crying for attention and research. What is life? Not just the DNA molecular chain, which is but the micro-physical manifestation of something far more subtle. What brings life, intelligent life, into the body of the newborn babe? What is death? What is it that takes place when the breath stops and the heart ceases to beat? What, if anything, precedes birth? And what happens after death?

The Rosicrucians know and reveal a great deal on these fascinating subjects. As you have seen, they maintain that each human being is dual in nature, composed of a physical body which is informed and vitalized by an intelligent essence referred to as the soul personality, or simply the soul. The physical body is born, lives and dies, but the soul personality persists through many such physical lives, acquiring experience and knowledge in each. You may say "If I have lived before, why don't I remember it?" I can tell you it is probably a very good thing not to remember too much about the past. We have not always lived saintly lives. There is quite a good possibility you would be filled with shame and remorse at some of the things you have done and this would weigh you down and discolor your present outlook on life. Actually you do remember some things. We all do. The skills that come easily to you, certain aversions and fears, and what is described as an "instinctive" knowledge of law or medicine or music or art are all memories carried over from other lives. Would it surprise you to learn that Solomon, Origen and Akbar were all different physical manifestations of the same great soul personality?

Today there are so many recorded and well-substantiated instances of people who have recalled one or more past lives that it hardly seems necessary to argue the point. Professor Ian Stevenson of the University of Virginia has a collection of several hundred such cases. All of the news services such as Associated Press and United Press International have large files on the subject and most well known news magazines have dwelt at one time or another on this theme. These are not vague recollections. In each case the individual had a very clear memory of the life preceding the present, saw himself, or herself, as an adult and not a child, recalled names and places, described relatives and even led the researchers to the house and the very room which had formerly been occupied, and, I might add, much to the wonder of the husband or brother or daughter still alive when they heard the strange young child speak to them affectionately and call them by pet names.

A well-known national magazine recently carried the story of a young Burmese girl who clearly recalled her two previous lives, both in the same family. In this family, the paternal grandmother died in 1948. Approximately eight months after her death a boy was born to the father and his wife, their first child. The boy was sickly and died at the age of five of leukemia. Three years later in 1957 another child, a girl, was born to the parents. From the day she learned to talk she maintained she had been both her dead older brother and her grandmother who had died in 1948. The interviewer who studied the case was convinced of her sincerity, particularly when she, still a child of nine, frequently forgot herself and her place in the family and addressed her father as if he were indeed her son. In Burma and in most Asian countries distinct forms of address are used to denote seniority and status within the family, so this act in itself was unusual. Even without the use of words like "father" or "mother" or "son" it can be known by the form used whether an elder or a younger relative is being addressed.

Reincarnation—A Fact of Existence

So much has been written on this subject, all of it easily available, that I will not elaborate further on it here. Suffice to know that the majority of the people of the world has always regarded reincarnation as a fact of existence and now, at last, we in the Western world are gradually coming around to an acceptance of it. However, there is one interesting and dramatic true story I would like to share with you.

Early in the twenties, Nicholas Roerich, the well-known painter and writer, conceived the idea of creating an identifying flag or symbol to be flown over all cultural institutions. His purpose was twofold: first, the obvious, to have nations agree not to bomb or destroy the cultural institution that flew the flag and thus preserve the priceless works of art or literature it contained; second, and not so obvious, the idea that if a group of nations could agree to cooperate on just one subject, the common interest would draw them together and provide a doorway to a much closer and more friendly relationship. He designed a flag consisting of three red circles in a white field and started a campaign to have the nations of the world adopt it.

This, it developed, was no easy task. Every bureaucracy thrives on red tape and this was particularly true of the governments which then existed in Europe and Asia. However, he was more successful in this hemisphere and, sensing an opportunity to align all American republics with his plan, he asked a friend and cultural associate of his wife and himself to undertake a mission to Argentina, Uruguay and Peru, the only Latin nations of South America that had not until then agreed.

This young woman was a person of character and considerable achievement. She was the editor of a nationally circulated magazine, a linguist, a writer and a concert pianist. She had been brought up in New Mexico, had a Spanish-speaking nurse as a child and spoke Spanish like a Mexican or South American. In fact, wherever she traveled in Latin countries they never took her for a "gringo." Always they considered her a Latin, like themselves, not of their country, perhaps, but of another Latin country nearby. In Mexico she was thought to be Venezuelan, in the Argentine they thought her Peruvian, and so on. Thus she was well qualified to meet and talk with the heads of state in the countries she was to visit.

Some years before, as part of her training, her Teacher had

disclosed to her that in a former life she had been Jean Philippe Rameau, a French musician of the 18th Century who is regarded as the father of certain musical theories held to the present day. She was naturally possessed of a great deal of musical knowledge and skill and wished to make music her life work but her Teacher, seeing her best growth potential lay in other fields of endeavor, told her of her musical history and pointed out it was not advisable for her to retrace that path.

Because she was impressed with the high purpose of the "Banner of Peace" plan, she accepted the mission and set sail for London in midsummer, 1933. In those days there was no direct passenger service between New York and Buenos Aires and the best way was through London and from there by ship to the Argentine. On the way she had much time for thought, and naturally had many misgivings about her ability to accomplish such a monumental task, a task which had already been given up by our own State Department. But she resolved to do what she could and stay there until she got agreement or refusal.

The ship docked in Buenos Aires on October 23, 1933. Imagine her surprise when on leaving the pier and entering the city she saw on all sides huge banners and signs which read RAMEAU! What a thrill! She found later that the people of Buenos Aires, a music-loving city, were celebrating the 250th anniversary of the birth of Rameau, but she could not help regarding it as a good omen for her mission. Coincidence—maybe. But it gave her confidence and so strengthened her resolve that she was successful and not long afterward all 21 American republics, including the United States, signed the Pact of the Banner of Peace.

Before Birth, the Soul Personality Selects Its Future Life

Now to continue about birth: Before the soul personality is ever assigned to, or attracted to a definite physical body and before the birth of that body, it has the privilege of reviewing the possibilities which may be offered by the life to come. Each life offers certain opportunities for development, for learning, for expanding the consciousness, for working out past karma and for moving ever closer to the proper and full expression of that particular God-quality selected by the soul prior to its very first incarnation in a physical form. Each one of us is working toward a certain aspect of perfection, a certain Beauty which we have glimpsed in the aura of God Himself and which we are ever seeking to reproduce here on earth. Our many lives here on this planet are testimony to the difficulty of the task to which we set ourselves so many, many years ago. To achieve our objective we asked for permission to use certain energies, the raw material with which we work, and we were granted these energies on the condition that we return them in as pure a state as they came to us. To our dishonor and unhappiness we allowed ourselves to be led astray from our original and most worthy objective and in so doing we corrupted, changed and soiled the energies which we had borrowed.

Today you are treading the path back to the Creator. You are beginning to correct the mistakes you have made and to restore the energy you have altered and changed. I am sure it is your intention to pay these debts and to draw together once again the threads you have torn. But you, and all of us, still continue of necessity to use psychic energy. With each breath we draw into our bodies and our auras fresh, clean, pure, unsullied energy which we intend to employ unselfishly and impersonally. But, as you know, even now in spite of best intentions you frequently slip and create more problems by the misuse of this energy.

This looks like an endless circle, a maze from which we could never extricate ourselves. And, indeed, we could not were it not tor the help we receive from Beings more advanced than ourselves who self-sacrificingly devote their time and life-energy to this task. Thus before coming into a physical body, every one of us is given the opportunity of observing several possible future lives each embodying certain lines of endeavor and certain possibilities for paying our debts. Usually the advanced soul will select the most difficult existence, not the easiest. This is because from his viewpoint in the spiritual realm the primary objective is to pay off debts and free himself from obligations as quickly as possible. But usually this is not permitted, for there is the ever-present danger that the load prove too heavy for the physical-emotional nature and result in a breakdown which will do more harm than good. The "wind must ever be tempered to the shorn lamb." Of course not every soul personality takes this ascetic attitude. In fact, only a few attempt to travel this Spartan path. Most seek only to reincarnate at the first opportunity without caring what possibilities await. Their only desire is to get back into a physical body not in order that they may advance, but to experience once again the violent emotions of both pleasure and pain that accompany all physical-plane life. Still others, but few in number, have a tendency to shy away from the physical and try to remain overlong in the psychic realm. These are eventually forced into incarnation for their own good, but without their having any voice in the selection of time, place and family environment. But I think I can say with assurance that the very fact you are now reading these words is an indication your spiritual development is such that you have actually selected the body you now have, the opportunities that have presented themselves and the life you are now leading. And what is more, you are making and remaking your life from day to day right now. You may be conscious of this or you may be acting without quite realizing where your compulsions come from, but there is a great probability you have altered your life stream and life opportunities at least once since your birth. This is true of everyone interested in learning more about the body and in improving one's capacity for understanding. This consecration to the idea of self-development and the broadening of consciousness causes your life to take a new turning, to present new opportunities for working off old karma and to open doors to a new understanding of life and its Creator. It is almost like being born again into a whole new life replete with new opportunities. Most of you who read this have done this at least once and some two or three times. The Master Jesus referred to this in the words, "You must be born again of water and the Holy Ghost." The Christian churches symbolize this in the sacrament of Baptism, using water and invoking the power of the Holy Ghost. But you have performed this miracle for yourself and may do so again. The clues are a new direction, a rededication, so to speak, involving a decision on your part.

As we have seen, the soul personality of a developed person like yourself faces at birth the need to choose one of several possible lives. None of these may be completely adequate to your need or previous development. There are not too many well-balanced marriages producing well-balanced bodies and sometimes a highly developed soul will be forced to accept a body which will burn out and break down under the power of energies which it is not equipped to sustain. As has been said, the advanced soul, eager to be of service, will gladly take this risk but sometimes it is not permitted and a more limited life is projected, one which offers a better possibility of success. So the soul personality eventually decides upon a certain future and is thereupon attracted to the physical embryo that will lead it into that future.

This soul will hover over the mother and attempt to guide her and guard her until the child is born. At birth, with the child's first breath, it enters the body and the newborn babe becomes a person—a living soul. Wordsworth says it comes "trailing clouds of glory" and indeed one frequently can see the peace and serenity of a great influence upon the faces of the smallest infants. For the first few weeks the soul personality retains a good recollection of its life in the psychic world and the events leading up to its birth in the new body. But the new physical equipment is unfamiliar and does not respond. It tries to talk and only strange sounds issue forth from its mouth. It hears, but nothing makes sense. It sees, but the eyes are not yet under control, half the time they are out of focus and even when they accidentally do focus directly upon some object, its size and dimensions are uncorrelated with the sense of touch and are meaningless. Thus, after a few weeks of struggling to understand its new equipment, the newly born person finally slips into the dream state of babyhood, and not until a year or so later does it gradually emerge as a new personality.

The ensuing lifetime presents the opportunity of paying the debts incurred in previous lives and of permitting others to repay you for your help to them. These debts must be repaid and the energy purified at the level at which the original misapplication occurred. Thus, physical violence of the past must be balanced off by physical suffering, an emotional upset like hate must be balanced by love and mental errors of vanity or pride must be balanced by humility. In this manner is the energy which was loaned to the struggling soul purified and returned to its Divine Source, freeing the individual of any further need to meet and cope again with the outward manifestation of that form of energy. Thus gradually do we free ourselves from the ties that bind us to this physical existence. When finally the last debt has been paid and the last bit of energy purified, we are free to leave the planet and return no more. We then need never again reincarnate in a physical body. Some will take advantage of this opportunity and move on to other worlds; a few, with the example of the unselfish help and service of the Great Mahatmas of this planet fresh in their minds, will decide to stay on here and help their struggling brothers and sisters. This work may be performed either in a physical body or from the etheric level without a physical counterpart.

But, alas, in spite of the high resolve and good intentions of the soul-personality before birth, the physical envelope is often weak and fails to live up to the standards set by the soul. Fresh new energy is petitioned and obtained and unfortunately it is frequently misused, so that at the end of the life span but little forward progress has been made. This means another round of death, instruction and rebirth for the soul personality.

What Happens at Death

At death most people fall into a deep slumber which is most restful and enables them to forget much of the unpleasantness and tension of life. Low-grade entities usually retain consciousness and fight to get back into a physical body as soon as they possibly can. On the other hand, the advanced student will proceed in full consciousness away from the earth plane and up to the higher realms. Actually, when souls pass through transition they are in various states of consciousness. The highly developed soul, the conscious chela of a Master and the advanced student pass over in full waking consciousness and are usually met by their own Master or a High Being sent at His direction to minister to them. They are quite eager to present themselves immediately to the Board of Judgment, so-called, and frequently these chelas and their Sponsors may do so within as little as twelve hours after transition. This is not a judgment in the sense that the life is adjudged to be a success or failure and corresponding reward or punishment meted out. No such thing. This Board is composed of at least three (and sometimes more) highly developed Entities with computer-like minds that assess and evaluate every single thought, emotion and action of the entire life, even the very smallest and most insignificant. Then, based upon this evaluation, the future training and instruction of the soul is determined, its place, its type and its duration. This is something an advanced student is most anxious to know; hence his eagerness to appear for this appraisal as soon as possible.

However, most souls on passing from the body are given what is called a "spiritual vacation," a release and relief from the pressures of life. The average individual, anticipating a reunion with departed members of the family and friends, is given every opportunity to visit with these loved ones for a certain period of time, to renew associations and to enjoy the happiness which they have been taught to expect. Some, however, are greatly surprised. The self-consciously religious who see themselves as paragons of virtue actually expect, when they come to realize they are dead, that they should be ushered into a glorious place of light accompanied by a fanfare of drums and trumpets. When they discover they are no different from before, or not very much, and when they find that no one pays attention to them except perhaps to pity them, they actually feel resentful. I dwell upon these types because they are numerous and also because they themselves and most of their family and friends fully expect that upon dying they will immediately be ushered in pomp before the throne of God. A person who is morally weak or frankly evil usually sees himself quite clearly and is ready for some sort of chastisement or rebuke, but those who believe themselves to be saints on earth expect reward. During their lifetime these people are often mentally and sometimes loudly critical of others. This, added to their complacent self-approval, creates a dull-appearing shell about them, which when seen by the inner eye has a shabby appearance that stays with them after death. Simple people with love in their hearts shine radiantly and the contrast is readily marked.

Most people have an erroneous idea of what constitutes good action and meritorious thought. They are impressed with the exterior signs of virtue and assume that if they appear to be "good, God-fearing people" they will have lived a proper life. In other words, they are more concerned with the image they present and what other people think of them than they are with their own progress.

You must learn to see yourself clearly, not through the eyes of others or your own astigmatic vision but through the eyes of your soul. Possibly the greatest concern of your soul right now is that you avoid giving injury to others and to yourself. You can injure by thought and by emotion as well as in physical action, probably more so. If you can achieve harmlessness, true harmlessness, in this life you will not have lived in vain.

As has been indicated, this Judgment Board is not sitting there waiting to mete out punishment. This erroneous impression has been created by certain organized religions which teach that upon death each person must face judgment and then be sent to either heaven or hell. Nothing could be more mistaken. The main thought and intention of this Board is to find a way by which each soul may be given the greatest possible opportunity to balance out its debt to life and learn how to control energy so that it may complete its evolution. Probably the worst experience of the newly departed soul, and the experience which may come nearest to the hell of the religious teachings, is the feeling of remorse and regret it suffers as it stands in the freedom of the etheric body and looks back at what it might have accomplished yet failed to do.

This Board acts at all times for the good of the individual and for the best interests of the entire human evolution. After the advanced soul and the Board have together examined the life just passed and assayed how near it came to attaining plans and promises made before birth, a decision is jointly reached. Usually, the soul's decision is much too severe and must be tempered by the mercy and farsighted vision of the Board. The soul then sets to work at inner levels to expiate as much of its karma as possible in the astral world. There is nothing painful in this. For the aspiring one it is a joyful service and fills him with a sense of accomplishment. Yet this is the very stage referred to by some religions as Purgatory. Many think of it as a place of punishment, yet the opposite is nearer the truth.

The foregoing applies to the advanced soul, the accepted chela or disciple. When the average man passes through transition he is usually allowed a certain time to rest and it is during this period of adjustment that contact with loved ones, father, mother, wife or husband, who have passed on before is permitted. They explain the characteristics of the "new" milieu to him and help bring about more quickly his understanding of and adjustment to it. When he is ready, and sometimes this is only after a passage of many years, he is called to come before the Board of Judgment. Usually he responds immediately, but he need not. This is a matter of individual decision. There are some who prefer to stay in the dream state of the astral realm and refuse to face up to the reality of future need and growth. They thus delay their own evolution until such time as they tire of the pleasures they have created for themselves.

Going still farther down the scale you find those who are convinced there is no existence after death and refuse to recognize one. These and certain sluggish-minded individuals fall at death into a deep sleep which may last a long time, sometimes several hundred years. They have no awareness of this passage of time but all the while a healing and nourishing process is at work on them. They awake finally in a refreshed state and are much more willing to take the necessary steps leading toward their own development.

Still farther down the scale there are those souls that are earthbound. These are individuals with such a strong love or such a powerful hate for the things of Earth or the people of Earth that they fight death and even after death refuse to believe they are not still alive. They cling to people or things they loved, or disliked, and live on the vitality and magnetism of living people. These types tend to reincarnate at the very first opportunity, usually quite recklessly, and thus create for themselves another chaotic existence.

A case that came to my attention some years ago may be of interest. I had known this man in life. He was handsome and charming and traded upon these qualities. Yet he had a keen intelligence and had become quite successful in business while still fairly young. But he loved night life and cafe society and succeeded in acquiring a reputation as a playboy. When the United States entered World War II in 1941, he took up his commission in the Navy and became one of the first U.S. casualties when his ship was torpedoed and sunk early in 1942. About the time the news of his death was released, I encountered him in the astral realm. He was one of a party in a night club, a very real-appearing creation of his own desire, and had no notion he was already dead in the physical sense. It was permitted to me to see him once or twice a month from then on. Each time he was drinking and dancing and joking and flirting in cafe society surroundings, fully convinced that the places and people were real and that he was still among the so-called living.

But after about three years he began to think. From time to time he would observe my presence, although at first he had not, and when he did, he would give me an anxious, worried look. It was obvious he was unhappy, so I petitioned help for him and it was granted. I found him sitting, as usual, in a fashionable night club. He was alone at a table which was covered with half-empty glasses and the usual debris to be found after a long evening. When I spoke to him he seemed to be in a stupor and it was difficult to get his attention. Even though there is no such thing as intoxication on the astral plane, he appeared to be in the apathetic condition of a man who has been drinking heavily for a long time Finally, I succeeded in rousing him and he looked directly at me and called me by name.

I said, "Steve, I want to help you. Do you know you are dead?"
Dumbly, he nodded slowly and then said, "I have been think-

ing so for some time. But I don't seem to be dead. Nothing much is changed. I'm so confused."

"I understand, Steve. You think this is just a bad dream and that soon you will wake up and find yourself in bed with a hangover."

He brightened. "Yes, that's just it. But if I am dead, what shall I do? It doesn't seem right, somehow, to go on like this."

So I told him what had been authorized. "You have to make a decision. It is entirely up to you. You have been reliving the existence which appealed to you most and up till now you have seemed to prefer that to any other. If you really want to get out of this repeating pattern, if you want to do something better and make something of value of yourself, you can do so by an act of your will, by making a decision, an honest decision. The opportunities will then develop."

He nodded to show he understood and then disappeared completely as the room slowly dissolved. I never saw him again. There was no need.

The events after transition are different for each individual and depend upon the state of consciousness and previous training. Some go to higher realms and are ecstatically happy while they study and are trained there. Some live in surroundings they have dreamed of living in, a creation of their desires while alive. This may be a cabin in the forest, a home on a beautiful farm, a cottage by the sea—in other words a heaven of their own making. But even this palls and after a time they usually seek to go higher. Some resent death and refuse to accept the idea. With every resource at their command they try to stay at earth level and participate in the physical life of others. Their one idea is to reincarnate in another body as soon as they can. Occasionally they succeed, bringing sorrow on the parents and greater trouble to themselves. Sometimes these lives are cut short at an early age, a merciful act, and this accounts for certain inexplicable deaths of infants and children. Eventually all come again to the need for rebirth and the process starts all over again. Between incarnations, the soul-personality is nourished, trained and improved so that at birth it is in a relatively high vibratory state and capable of great things. You have noticed, I am sure, that the average youngster is a pretty fine person and it is only as he grows older and is exposed to the bad example of his elders and the many temptations that beset his path that his standards slip and his character and abilities degenerate.

I urge you therefore to protect children, your children, all children. Guard them in the privacy of your home as well as publicly in the schools, playgrounds and other meeting places where children group together. When young they are highly telepathic and respond most sensitively to every thought and emotion of those close to them. In many cases these responses are far surer and more deep-seated than those you urge upon them with your words. Therefore it is well that you watch your thoughts and temper your emotions when you are near them. Bathe them in love and give them confidence in you and in themselves and they will grow strong and beautiful like flowers in the sunshine.

Have you noticed that the second child in a family frequently doesn't learn to talk as quickly as the first? You would expect it to be the other way around. The answer is that the second child doesn't have the same need to talk. The older brother or sister knows his wants and needs and tells the parents, "Sissy wants you to pick her up," the older one will explain, or "Jo-jo wants his ball." The sounds uttered by the baby are incomprehensible to an adult but very easily understood by a toddler not too much older. This is telepathic attunement.

There is usually quite a noticeable rapport between mother and small child. Unfortunately many mothers who respond psychically to the needs of their children seldom realize that the child is in turn responding to their adult emotions. How many times have you seen mothers with foolish fears hand them on to their children—the fear of snakes, of lightning, of burglars, even fear of the dark. Psychiatrists know now that many of the unreasonable fears and prejudices we harbor today were implanted in our consciousness by our elders when we were infants and small children. They are deep-seated and extremely difficult to uproot and they account for many strange things people do without really knowing why.

How to Recall Past Lives

Rosicrucians are taught how to recall past lives. No previous life ever comes back in complete detail, any more than you can recall the details of your present life. But certain events which have left an outstanding impression or which have a bearing on the present life are frequently remembered. One member has succeeded in bringing recollections of many previous lives. Some may be of interest to you so I will repeat them, using his own words.

> These life impressions go pretty far back in time. The earliest as far as I can figure out was when I belonged to a very primitive tribe of people. The experience was at night. It was quite dark and the only light came from torches which gave off almost as much smoke as light. In the dim glow I was aware of thirty or forty men near me but there were more, I was sure of that. The excitement was intense. There was a jubilation in it too. Apparently we had achieved a victory, a very important victory of some sort, and were returning in a triumphant procession. I felt very strong and agile and was jumping up and down brandishing a long wooden spear. Like the others, I was completely nude.

This member tried to assemble his experiences in some sort of chronological order. There is no certainty he is correct, because at no time did he see a calendar. They did not occur sequentially, so his conclusions were drawn from the appearance of dress and circumstances.

> This second experience is difficult to place but I think it is remote in time. I stood in a small room with stone walls. Beyond the doorway was a much larger room in which there were a great many people. To judge from the rush of sound created by the whispered voices and rustles of clothing, it was a large gathering. Two oriental-looking people were dressing me, one a man about sixty, small and wiry with a wrinkled face topped by a head of close-cropped gray hair. The other was a small, dark, rather plump woman. They lifted a single

white one-piece garment high and put it on over my head. It appeared to be like a white cotton or silken tube of fairly light material which went to the floor and had openings at the top for my head and two arms. The man then put a single stole-like garment around my neck so that the ends hung down in front across my chest. This was made of heavily embroidered silk. The woman brought a long gold chain, which she proceeded to fasten around my waist. At each end of the chain was a curiously worked golden triangle and these were used as clasps to hold the chain snugly about me. The two then stood back and surveyed me carefully and when apparently satisfied, the man brought a metal bar or tube, heavily ornate, with a chased metal surface and heart-shaped protuberances at each end. This he placed in my right hand and said, "Now you are ready." At that, I turned and started through the doorway to the larger room, and the experience ended.

The most precious of all lives to me and one to which I return many times in recollection was quite a simple one. Apparently I was a monk or some sort of religious (person). All scenes from this life, and there have been many, occur in the same place, a small room which looks out on the sea. Sometimes it is morning, sometimes late afternoon, sometimes dark night, but always I am in the same room, a room which I love. It is a most simple room and quite small. The walls are of stone and the window which is high above the rocks and sea below is eternally open, with no way to cover or close it. In the room is a narrow bed, a table and one straight-backed wooden chair. In the corner is a chest in which my meager possessions, mostly books, are kept. I look out of the window at the waves dashing on the rocks below, I smell the salt spray and hear the cries of the sea gulls as they wheel and turn before me. This room I love. It fits me like a glove and I feel warm and happy there.

I remember many deaths. Some painful, some slow and lingering, some sudden. At times I was a woman, but more often a man. In one particularly horrible death I was a woman, a young girl, a virgin. It must have been in Roman times because the soldiers that vanquished our city wore a sort of primitive armor. One huge brute entered our home and taking me by the hair hauled me into a bedchamber. With blows he forced me onto a low bed-like structure and began to assault me. The pain in my loins was great but the disgust and humiliation were greater. His breath was foul and the armor, which he did not bother to remove, cut into the soft skin on my breast and stomach. As he reached his climax his head came close to mine and I seized his ear in my mouth. Biting hard and with a quick jerk of my head I tore the ear right off. In fury he raised up and taking a short mace which he carried as a sidearm, struck me on the head. With the second blow I expired.

There were many other life experiences, often quite commonplace and somewhat similar one to the other except for the surroundings. A complete tabulation would fill many books, but I will relate just two more, one because of its vivid realism and the other because it had a bearing on my present life. The vivid experience must have been a life lived in the United States in early Colonial days. It started in a room in which there were about twenty women and as many small children. The women were of all ages and dressed quite plainly. Over the entire room and all the people in it hung a pall of fear so thick you could almost slice it. I was a man, that I knew, and it was up to me to do something, but I didn't know what. So I decided I would find my sidekick, my partner, and he and I would try to work out some solution. I left the room and walked along a muddy street. The sun was out and there were people walking about. Two parallel boards over the thick mud made walking a little easier and I noticed that as I walked along on these narrow planks that everyone I encountered stepped aside into the mud to let me pass.

Whether this was in fear or in respect I do not know. At the time I had only one thought—how to save these women and children and this village from the fate which apparently threatened. What this threat was never became clear in my mind. It was there and I took it for granted. As I walked along I kept a sharp eye open for my partner. I looked in various doorways and called a question to one or two people.

Finally I entered a dim doorway and went up a flight of stairs covered by a carpet which was now so saturated with mud and water it had hardened to a crust. The stairs led into a large room which had a bar all along the far side. Before the bar stood my partner and to my utter dismay I saw he would be no help at all. He was dead drunk. He was dressed in blue jeans and boots. He had on a dirty blue cotton shirt with long sleeves and a leather vest. Tipped onto the back of his head was a large hat. Around his waist were two cartridge belts ending in holsters with guns on each hip. But he was harmless and helpless, because he was so drunk he couldn't stand and was shamelessly hanging onto the bar. With a shrug at the hopelessness of the situation I walked to the bar and ordered whisky. As I raised the glass to toss it down I caught sight of myself in the fly-specked mirror and was amazed to see I was almost a replica of my drunken pal, same hat, same vest, same guns and a lean, weather-browned, wrinkled face, old beyond its years. The raw whisky scorched my throat and the experience ended as suddenly as it had begun, an unexplained and unresolved vignette from a life I have no other clues to.

These episodes have all come to me during meditative periods at the start of which I petitioned for knowledge of previous lives as instructed in the Rosicrucian monographs. Each one was but a picture, a part of a story and most had no introduction and no ending. The last I will include here is one which had a profound influence on my present life. It was experienced some years ago while I was still a bachelor. At that time no thought of marriage had entered my head but I knew and entertained about ten or twelve different young women of my own age. All were attractive and intelligent, each had her own charm and appeal. The experience was quite unexpected and came as a shock. I was in the act of leaving a house. I had on a hat and coat and was carrying a small hand case. As I turned to the door a young woman dressed in a white housecoat-type of garment, all lace and frills, came hurrying down a broad staircase into the hall where I stood. She had been crying and her face was anguished.

'Don't go, darling,' she cried, 'It's all my fault.'

I knew it was not her fault but my own. Being too cowardly or too stupid to just state the real reason for my leaving her, I had trumped up a quarrel and made a scene pretending that I was going off in a temper. All I knew then was that I had to get away, to be alone and this urgency had led me to leave my wife. She threw herself into my arms and pressed her tear-wet cheek to mine and as she did so I knew her. I mean I knew her identity in my present life. She was one of the young women of my acquaintance, a very beautiful and desirable young woman.

In a flash all became clear. I had broken off a life with this soul and now was being given the privilege of resuming it in order that it might be properly finished and its original purpose carried out. I sought out this woman, paid court to her, fell in love with her again (it was easy), found she loved me, married her and we have been most happy ever since. To my mind this was the most helpful and most fortunate of all my life recollections.

The foregoing will give you some idea of the form in which fragments of previous lives are usually recalled. This man's experiences are quite like those of other students. He has spent more time and effort in trying to recall past lives and therefore his results have been fuller and more complete. Most students, after one or two such experiences which satisfy them that they have actually lived before, lose active interest and turn their attention to the more productive aspects of Rosicrucian work.

Astral Vision: Penetrating the Astral Veil

Today the wall between the seen and the unseen once again grows thin. Before too many years pass a great many people will discover they have what is called psychic sight or astral vision. This is the ability to see auras and to discern the forms of people and other entities which exist only on the etheric and astral levels. Today, some do possess this ability, but they have worked to develop it and trained themselves either in this life or in a previous one. But in days to come many more will gain it.

At one time all educated, trained and well-developed people possessed astral vision. This was several thousand years ago. They could see both the physical and, with a little extra effort, the next finer grade of matter. In this lies the origin of the ancient religion of the Chinese and other Asiatic peoples, that which is called ancestor worship. In those days the father of the family had great authority and he usually exercised it with wisdom and restraint. All major decisions were left to him and each member consulted with him and sought his advice in their personal affairs. Nearly every one of these patriarchs was keenly aware of the great responsibility for the welfare of his family which was thus placed upon his shoulders and he thought and worked to the best of his ability to discharge it with honor. When it came time for him to die, a special room was prepared in the home, a sort of shrine, which was devoted to the father alone. After death he would return daily in spirit to this shrine, where he could be seen by the elder members of his family, in order to give them advice and help. This was repeated until a son was trained and ready to take his place, and even after he had done so, the son would often repair to the shrine to consult with his ancestor.

As time moved on and the entire human race became more materially focused, people gradually lost the ability to penetrate the astral veil. But the Chinese continued the practice of revering and attempting to consult with their immediate ancestors on matters of importance. Most old-fashioned Chinese homes still contain such a shrine before which the devoted children and grandchildren offer their prayers. They no longer see the beloved departed one, but at one time they did and there will come a time, not too far in the future, when that vision will be returned to them.

It is possible for you to develop astral or psychic sight. This is but a matter of training, and in a subsequent chapter certain exercises and techniques will be given which will enable you to prove this for yourself.

Before concluding this chapter I would like to urge you to think at least once each day about those of your friends and loved ones that have already passed through transition. This is described by most religions as praying for the dead. We are all in this world together as parts of one great evolutionary process. No one can proceed along the path too far in advance of the rest. And in like manner a few delinquents can hold up the development of all others. But we can help some when they find it most difficult to help themselves. I refer to the time immediately after transition when, if willing and cooperative, the soul can be taught so much and trained so well. Pray for the departed ones, see them surrounded by light. Send them love and good thoughts on the wings of your life energy and you can be the means of lifting a soul-personality to a point where it will try to help itself. This great forward step can be accomplished with your help.

This is a task truly worthy of the efforts of an esoteric student. In performing this task, you help an individual to redeem itself, you help advance the evolution of the entire race and, most of all, you help yourself. This is a good work. Pray for the dead!

FOUR

The Power of Thought: First Steps to the Control of Your Destiny

When we are born, our physical brain is a blank, a page with nothing written upon it. "Naked and alone we come into exile —into the unspeakable and incommunicable prison of this earth," said Thomas Wolfe. He understood and described in colorful language the problem each of us faces at birth. Everything must be learned, everything is new. The infant has no skills, no trained brain cells, no thought and motion sequences to depend upon. It is capable only of those primitive reflex actions that are controlled by the lower part of the brain, crying when in pain or distress, smiling and gurgling when pleased. As the child develops, the upper part of the brain which was blank at birth begins to record, retain and correlate the observations of the senses. This is not unlike the programming of one of our modern computers. The muscles learn by trial and error to adjust to various requirements and a whole series of motion sequences is installed, ready to be called upon when needed.

The eye of the newborn has no perception of depth or distance. This must be learned by correlating vision with touch. The child must find out just how far and how fast to extend its arm in order to pick up a glass from the table. Then the restraining muscles which slow down the movement at the right distance must be taught or the glass will be knocked over. Also the proper tension of the fingers must be learned or the glass will fall. All these and a thousand other highly complex movements must be programmed into the new brain. This is a slow process which must be learned for each type of muscular action and it takes a long time, usually several years, before the growing child can demonstrate satisfactory control.

Physical competence is, of course, only the beginning. Next should come the disciplining of the emotions and the mind, but unfortunately most modern educators fail to accord this the importance it merits. True, home training and the need to "get along" in school and in business impose certain restraints, but no one today attains anything approaching the same control over emotions and mind that they display in the physical areas. This glaring human deficiency is at the heart of most of the present unrest, conflict and political disturbance. How can one presume to direct events when his own emotions and thoughts are permitted to run wild?

Have you thought of this? A person with an affliction like cerebral palsy is pitied for his obvious lack of physical control, and one who lazily or through ignorance fails to develop elementary physical skills is an object of contempt. Should not similar value be placed upon emotional and mental discipline? The Rosicrucians believe so and their training program, which is given here in capsule form, is designed to help you gain this control. They recommend that one proceed step by step in an orderly fashion not too unlike the gradual learning process of the small child. Processes similar to the motion sequences established in the brain of the child must be built into the mind by thought.

Thought Is the Greatest Energy

It has been stated often, and quite truly, that thought is the greatest energy. History relates again and again how the destiny of mankind has been altered by new ideas, by the powerful thoughts of original thinkers. The vision of a united world led Alexander, Caesar, Genghis Khan, Napoleon and more recently

Hitler into their wars of conquest—a great idea badly carried out. The vision still persists and probably will become eventually the guiding influence in the creation of world peace but via a voluntary instrument like the United Nations, rather than a forced submission. It is clear also that the scientific progress of our world today, with its luxuries and comforts, is the result of thought. The remarkable achievements of cooperative effort, evidenced in the efficiency of our great industrial and commercial complexes, are due to the creative thinking of the men who planned these companies.

Miracles Can Be Accomplished by the Energy of Thought

Yes, no one will deny that thought is powerful and most will admit it is the most powerful energy available to man. For this reason it is easy to accept as true a statement that miracles can be accomplished by thought, that thought can change your life, bring you wealth, comfort, security, whatever you need and want. And it can, if you know *how* to think.

Many students become confused and discouraged when they try to use the energy of thought and fail to attain the desired objective. They may read or be told, "Concentrate upon success, visualize yourself enjoying the success you desire," or again in another vein, "Raise your consciousness to God and you will find peace and happiness." These admonitions are sound and true but for the average person they are equivalent to having someone point to a piano and say, "Play Rachmaninoff's Second Piano Concerto and it will calm your nerves." This may be good advice but all three of these injunctions presume a training and skill which few possess and therefore it is not surprising that most of us fail when we try to do as they suggest.

In order to employ the power of thought it is necessary to start from the beginning and learn to use your mind and brain in almost the same way the infant achieves control of his muscles. The child learns automatically, driven by its needs and desires. You must consciously train yourself, a more difficult task because it requires the use of the will.

The Powers of Observation

In the Rosicrucian technique one starts by training the powers of *observation*. This method was used and recommended by Gautama Buddha as an initial step in training the mind. He would walk among His students while lecturing them, then suddenly stop and ask, "Where was I standing when I uttered the word faith?" Or at another time He would pause in His instruction and say, "What movements did I make with my right hand when I spoke of beauty?" Thus He taught His pupils attentiveness and trained their powers of observation. Here are three exercises designed as initial steps in learning to use your mind. They are quite simple, so simple you may think to yourself, "How can this help me?" Do not discount them. Your mind has a vast potential and until you learn how to tap this tremendous reservoir of power you will not realize to even a small degree on your capabilities. These exercises are the first step. They are designed to help you learn to "take hold of a thought." Practice each one of them at least once a day from now on. It will be no hardship —they take but a few seconds—and before long they will become almost habitual. Here are the exercises. You can see how simple they are.

1. When you go into a room for the first time, shut your eyes for a second and see how many objects in the room you can name—table, chairs, pictures, ashtrays, desks, whatever you can recall. Do this whenever you enter a room or any place new to you.

2. After ascending or descending a flight of steps, recall how many there were.

3. (This to be done in the evening only.) Recall what you did when you first left the house this morning—or if you did not leave, what you did after breakfast. What did you see? What did you do? Recall about three or four minutes of this activity, no more. The next day recall what you did after lunch or in any other three-minute interval of your day.

After two or three weeks daily practice of the foregoing you
will begin to grasp their purpose and probably will design some
similar exercises of your own. As you notice, the third exercise
is slightly different from the others and is a step into a higher area
of training. As I have said—don't let the obvious simplicity of
these formulae deceive you; don't underrate them. They provide
an essential preliminary training without which no sound mental
control can be developed.

The Powers of Concentration

The next step toward mind control is training in *concentration.* Just as I am sure many of you said to yourselves, "I don't
need these exercises in observation, my powers of observing are
already well enough developed," so I am sure a certain number
of you will say, "I don't need to learn to concentrate. I can concentrate just fine on anything I want. My whole business (or my
whole life) demands concentration and I have had to learn this."
You will get no argument from me on your abilities. You may
have the keen, highly trained observation powers of a big-city
detective or you may possess the ability to concentrate of an
atomic scientist, but you miss the point. The purpose of these
exercises is to teach you how to lay hold on thought, how to "find
the handle," as the baseball players say. They differ from the
normal, everyday type of observation and concentration in that
they are conscious deliberate acts of the will and not the automatic result of a compelling need. There is a difference between
emotionally motivated thought and thoughtfully motivated emotion which I will discuss later in this chapter, but now here are
some exercises in concentration. These should be performed at
least once each day and you can start them the same day you
start the observation exercises. You can employ them concur-
rently or not, as you see fit.

1. Multiply two numbers of two digits each (such as 26 and
   39) in your head—not with pencil and paper. Do this until
   you are sure your answer is correct. Then do the same with

two numbers of three digits each (as 413 x 765). Do this once each day with different numbers.

2. Memorize four lines of a poem, any poem, long or short. Do this once a day. These exercises need not go on forever, but they should continue until you begin to understand what is meant by "taking hold of thought."

3. When passing people in the street or any other place where you can see a person for a short time and then have him pass out of your field of vision, select one person and look closely into his face. Then look away and for one minute or more hold that face (a picture of it) in your mind's eye. Study its expression. Seek to understand its owner.

As you realize, exercise number 3 is different from 1 and 2 and you are correct in assuming it is designed to lead you a step beyond what you now know and understand. A conscientious practice of this exercise will be found very rewarding. Without any special effort on your part, you will find that you are developing a capacity for attuning with the people whose faces you hold before you. You will become aware of their dominant emotions—very often fear because today many people are fear-ridden, less often pity or compassion, sometimes joy, sometimes anger. If you are sensitive and pursue this practice for a longer period you will gradually become aware of their thoughts—or better, their thought forms.

Your conscious application to these exercises puts your brain to work in such a simple way that you can observe it working. Then by observation of your brain at work, you will gradually come to an apprehension of thought. Thought is an activity of your mind and the mind can function apart from the brain. Thus it is possible to think apart from the brain and certain people have trained themselves to do this. But the average person is trained from birth to recognize only those impacts upon his consciousness that come via the physical senses and record themselves on his brain. Thus all scientific thought, deductions based upon physical observations, and all reasoning are done through the brain. Almost all of the memory records you use are stored in brain tissue. Your mind keeps a much better memory storehouse than the brain but because we lean so heavily on the brain we seldom reach into the mind to recall an incident from the past. We are all so dependent on the brain that even abstractions like love, hate, fear, patriotism, and generic ideas like dog, horse, house, and farm—which are clearly superphysical and therefore belong in the realm of the mind—even they register or employ a corresponding image in the brain or on that inner screen of the brain sometimes called the phantasm.

The Powers of Meditation

If you want to use thought to its full potential, if you want to employ the great power of thought, you must learn to think consciously apart from the brain. The brain is a wonderful and most useful tool but for most creative work, creation of the highest order, the brain is like a strait jacket which restricts, binds and limits the action of the mind. So it is necessary to go on to another group of exercises designed to aid you in your effort to employ thought consciously and with purpose. These are exercises in *meditation*.

As you undoubtedly realize, concentration exercise 3 is partly meditative in character There are many meditation techniques which differ one from the other according to need and purpose. Here we will give three exercises all aimed at the same objective, to train you to apprehend and employ thought.

1. Find a place where you will be free from interruption for five minutes Seat yourself in a straight back chair with your feet touching but not crossed. Allow your hands to rest easily in your lap and sit relaxed but with your back straight and your head erect. Breathe easily and naturally. Close your eyes and think of the color blue, any shade of blue from the pale blue which is nearly white all the way down the scale to the deep purple. Think of just one shade in any one meditative period. See it all around you. See it fill the entire room. Do not dwell on this for more than one minute but at the same time do not let your mind wander. This will require an effort of the will and you may not be entirely

successful at first, but keep trying and you will be. When the minute (approximately) is up, spend the next minute thinking of pink and the third minute in the same manner thinking of pure white, the white of new-fallen snow in the sunshine, a crystalline brilliance. Spend not more than three minutes in all, then rise, take a deep breath and relax. Then proceed to the next meditation.

2. Resume the same position as in exercise 1 and with your eyes closed, think of a sound. Think of a violin playing— playing any selection familiar to you. But it must be a violin, not voice or another musical instrument. If an orchestration should swell up around the key sound, separate it out until you hear only the clear note of the violin. One minute only For the next minute hear a horn or a reed instrument like a saxophone, either one. But remember, hear only that one instrument and shut out all other sound. For the third minute hear in your mind a piano playing a piece of music familiar to you. This is more difficult because instead of single notes there will be chords and complex combinations. Carry it for a minute, not more, then shut it out, rise, take a deep breath and relax.

As you can observe, these are training exercises. They parallel in the area of the mind the simple movements of the infant who is exploring the physical world for the first time. These are your initial endeavors to experiment with the mental world. To perform them perfectly is at first impossible. You will make many errors. You won't be able to carry the violin or piano clearly and other sounds will intrude well before the full minute has been completed. The colors will become confused and you will have a veritable rainbow at one time and no color at all at another. But gradually by trying and keeping at it you will gain more and more.

3. The third exercise is of a different type. In 1 and 2 you heard sounds and saw colors and your will was brought into play only in order to keep your attention upon the desired objective and to shut out disturbance. In this, the third exercise you are to use your will in a different way. So sit as

before and when you have relaxed with your eyes closed see the color pink all around you. See a clear light pink, not a fabric pink but pink as in a ray of light. It is important to see this not only in front and to the sides but also in back, above, below and all around you. See yourself entirely enveloped in a pink cloud which extends six to ten inches out from you in all directions. Hold this image for one full minute, then dismiss it from your mind, rise, take a deep breath and relax.

These are basic exercises, each one slightly different. Many variations exist; there are probably hundreds. As you progress you will catch the tone of each exercise and be able to design variations of your own. But for the present follow the outline given. Remember, in the world of the mind you are like a baby learning to walk or learning to hold things. Just as the infant programs into his consciousness the right muscular action to use when picking up a spoon, so you must learn the delicate control necessary to bring a thought form into physical manifestation.

At this point I want to reveal to you a little-known but very important fact. The mind is the kingly part of each one of us. It is designed by nature and the power it can wield to be the ruler of our lives and to control all the events in them. Yet most of us employ it as a servant. We make the mind the slave of our appetites and emotions. The mind accepts this indignity with considerable reluctance. It registers subtle complaints but, with our customary lack of awareness, we don't notice them. And we completely fail to understand its more vigorous protests which often take the form of illness and disaster. No wonder our attempts to use the power of the mind usually end in failure.

For the purposes of analysis we have been describing human nature as having three parts, the physical, emotional and mental. Actually, no separation or division exists. They are all you. Normally you think of the physical body as "I." This is the visible collection of cells and molecules known as John Smith or Sally Jones. It eats and breathes to keep its life and rests when it is tired. Its basic functions are mostly automatic and were designed by an Intelligence far above and beyond our creative abilities.

These physical bodies are most remarkable instruments. They have the ability to repair themselves and if allowed to function uninterruptedly in the smooth automatic manner in which they were designed, they would probably last forever—or at least as long as we wanted to use them. But humanity—and this means all of us—has developed certain habits of action and emotion and thought that interfere with the normal functioning of the physical equipment and cause it damage.

Today most intelligent and well-educated people control their physical impulses very well. We are beginning to learn the art of self-restraint. But unfortunately our emotional natures are still dominant and, in spite of our good intentions and best efforts, the emotional nature takes control and orders the "complete man" around. The great fears so rampant in the world—and in our present day the greatest sin is probably fear—infect nearly everyone. Fear, like several other basic emotions, is an incentive to action, a powerful incentive to physical action. Originally it was implanted for a good purpose. When fear was experienced, and primitive man only felt fear when confronted by danger, adrenalin was released immediately into his blood stream in order to stimulate his heart action and give him a rapid increase in strength and energy with which to meet the threat. Today we experience fear quite often when there is no danger present. Since the body does not analyze, it releases the adrenalin to provide strength and energy, which is then not used. This leaves a residue which becomes a poison in the bloodstream and eventually breaks down the physical structure, one way in which a destructive emotion can cause actual physical damage. There are countless others. It can be said without fear of contradiction that all violent emotions leave harmful physical effects in their wake.

To live on the emotional level, and most people today do live on the emotional level, to permit our emotions to control our actions seriously hampers the functioning of our minds. The emotions were designed as tools to be used, as incentives to action. We mistakenly let them rule us. If you would change this pattern, if you would improve your life and create a future nearer your heart's desire, take the first step upward. Learn how to think. Learn how to let your mind direct your life and displace the authority of your emotions.

Those who have tried this know it to be more difficult than it sounds. Yet it is not so difficult but that everyone who reads this may accomplish it. Determination, will and work are required. And the place to begin is with the simple exercises given earlier in this chapter. These will lead you step by step in a most gentle fashion away from emotional control and bring your mind into the dominant position for which it was designed.

Let me make some points clear. Your physical appetitites are not to be blocked out, they must not be negated. That is the way of suppression which always ends in an explosion. Control and guidance form the proper technique by means of which the physical impulse is redirected, rechanneled and not suppressed. For example, if you have a craving for a rich dessert which you know is not good for you, it is better to take something like fruit than nothing at all. In this way the craving is not denied, merely redirected to a better food. Some teachers recommend that you "kill out desire." This does not mean you should eliminate and destroy your emotions. You would be only half human if you did. Again, the best technique is redirection. Each emotion is dual in nature. It has higher and lower counterparts. You should strive to channel all your emotional drives into the higher counterparts. For example, we are told that love is the highest emotion of which we are capable, yet it has lower and higher counterparts —love of self as opposed to love of others. Brought to its highest, love of others becomes love of all men, nay, love of all that lives and breathes. As another example, fear is most destructive and must be replaced with trust and confidence. The higher counterparts are creative and will bring to you the strength and the benefits that you need. Each emotion should be examined, not taken for granted. If you are manifesting the lower counterpart, try to change it to its higher form.

It is unwise to attack the emotions directly. By doing so you focus your attention upon your desires and in this way they are actually strengthened, for energy follows thought. It is much better to approach the problem as has been suggested, by taking steps to develop an awareness of and an interest in your mind. As you become more and more preoccupied with your mental processes, your physical appetites and lower emotions will gradually lose their dominance over you, until you are ultimately able to free the power of thought. Therefore do not regard the exercises suggested here as trivial. They are simple, yes, but they are the first steps on the highway which leads to the control of your destiny.

FIVE

The Power of Thought: Physical-Etheric and Emotional Energy

In order to understand thought and how to use the power of the mind, you must first have a comprehension of energy. There are many kinds of energy. The most familiar is of course physical energy, whose grades and types are almost infinite. There are gravity and magnetism, light and heat, water power and air power, atomic energy and stellar energy and a thousand ramifications of each.

One of the most useful and fascinating of the physical energies is electricity. In its myriad forms electricity has changed our whole way of life. The telephone, the radio and television are dramatic evidences but there are many others just as important. For example, the electron microscope which has revealed the infinitely small and the radio telescope which brings to our vision the infinitely distant have expanded our universe millions of times over in the few years since their development.

These are all physical energies but, as you know, there are more subtle energies employed by man, human energies which are not obvious and consequently not so well understood. These are etheric, emotional, mental and psychic energies, each in progressively finer and more rapid vibratory states. Established science has very little to say about them and most of the meager information it offers is distorted by prejudice. The Rosicrucians have devoted a great deal of time to the study of energy but the amount of space available here does not permit the exhaustive exposition this subject deserves.

Etheric Energy

This is the energy which is nearest to physical energy. In fact it is the energy which living entities use to manipulate and move the physical, the energy which you use unconsciously when you work, or lift your arm, or turn your head. We live in a vast sea of life energy and we seine off small quantities for our own use. The life energy which vibrates at the slowest rate is etheric energy. Its accumulation and use by a human being is almost entirely automatic and well below the level of consciousness. However, through training you can learn to manipulate etheric energy. This is of value in the practice of physcial healing, which I will explain in detail in a later chapter. However, most students find it quicker and easier to go directly to the study of mental energy because when it is understood and brought under control, the etheric control becomes automatic.

Emotional Energy

It might be well before proceeding further to give a definition of energy. The dictionary describes energy as "the power by which anything acts effectively to move or change things or accomplish any result," or "power in active exercise," or more simply, "the capacity to perform work." It divides energy into "potential energy" and "kinetic energy." Anything in motion has kinetic energy, a moving automobile, a falling rock, a breaking wave. Potential energy is sub-divided into "available energy" and "diffuse energy." To explain this we might say a coiled clock spring contains available energy, while a lump of coal contains diffuse energy, the difference being that the coiled spring is ready for immediate work but the lump of coal must be burned before its energy is released in the form of heat.

All life energy is diffuse. It must be converted or transformed in some way in order to be put to work. Every human being has an array of energy transformers which enable him to draw upon the life energy which surrounds him and in which he lives, moves and has his being. The ancient Hindu or Sanskrit term for these transformers is chakras or wheels. This name comes from their appearance. To a person with psychic vision they look like rapidly spinning wheels of different-colored light. The raw life energy is pure and without any distinguishing characteristics but when it is transformed into human energy by one of these chakras, it takes on the quality of that particular transformer. The most fully opened and therefore most active chakra in average humans is the solar plexus, whose chief product is emotional energy. In consequence these people are "emotionally focused," which means that most of their actions are taken as the result of an emotional impulse or urge. Even some with very well-developed minds permit their better judgment to be swayed by the power of their emotions, when the reverse should be the case. For this reason there is built into each person a subconscious block to the full use of mental power until that person's emotions have been brought under the control of the mind. So right now, on our way to learning the power of thought, we will examine the emotions and learn how to use them to achieve our objectives.

Emotional Telepathy

Now let me tell you something very important about emotion. Except in certain rare and unusual situations only a small part of the emotion you feel is your own, that is to say, self-generated. The emotional world is like an ocean and our emotional bodies are like fish in it. Sometimes the sea is rough and we are disturbed and tossed about. At other times it is relatively calm and we feel serene. True, we are occasionally excited when all about us is quiet but on the other hand it is almost impossible to maintain equanimity with an emotional storm breaking over our heads. Emotions are quite easily transmitted from one person to another by a sort of emotional telepathic rapport. This is a study in itself which we will examine in detail in the chapter on telepathy.

To develop an awareness of the emotional surges and impulses that move us, we must first determine which are self-originated and which come from without. Sometimes the distinction is easy. Not too long ago I made a short journey by train. After settling myself in my seat I was surprised to observe that I was feeling indignation. Knowing full well I had no reason to feel indignant I sought for the cause. It was not hard to discover. All about me people were reading newspapers in which were stories of riots and looting which had that day taken place in a nearby city. It was their indignation and resentment which I felt—not mine. When a friend or a member of your family comes to you with a long face and a tale of grievance, don't accept the dubious emotional gift that is offered. That is her little quagmire. You can't help by jumping in. A certain amount of restraint and good judgment are needed. You need not be cold and unfeeling—just don't permit yourself to be carried along on the wave of the other person's emotion.

When you identify the emotion you feel as coming from without, in other words as not your own, it is not too difficult to dissociate yourself from it, if you want to. Let me emphasize those last four words—if you want to. Very often you will find the emotion pleasant, exciting or in some other way attractive and you won't want to give it up. But if you decide to separate yourself from an emotional wave that does not belong to you it is only necessary to step out of it. It is like stepping out of a shower, or out of a cloak or in some cases out of a room or cell. The separation can be complete, or only partial. It is for you to decide.

Popular opinion is a very powerful influence. As a rule this is emotionally keyed and you can divorce yourself from this inhibition as simply as you release yourself from the anger of a neighbor or the fears of a child. Just as you can be and are often affected by the unpleasant and violent emotions of others, so you may also benefit by contact with pleasant and loving emotional waves. You are well aware that many people lean on others and derive from the contact a certain emotional solace. It may happen also that another will try to help you, or his support may be given without his conscious realization. In any event, emotions seldom act at a distance and the closer the physical bodies are to each other the more powerful is the emotional transfer.

Your mind is more powerful than your emotions and it is your mind that must be used to cut away the unwanted emotional debris deposited by others and also to scalpel out your own undesirable emotions. You should use your mind as a tool and in a sense argue your way out of emotions that are unpleasant or harmful. When you feel fear, you should say to yourself, "What is there to fear? I am secure. This is not a new situation. I have faced it—or one like it—more than once without dire consequences. So why fear?" These are the first steps to be taken. It is not the will that is used. Use of the will leads to suppression and the danger of unexpected explosive outbreak. Use the mind. It can succeed in ridding you of the most obvious emotional burdens. The more subtle, such as pride, self-righteousness and vanity, are not so easily discovered. We often go for years without realizing that many of our decisions and actions are being guided by some such follies. But as we begin to clear our auras of the cloudier emotions these more subtle ones have a way of revealing themselves a little at a time. They are usually deeply ingrained and consequently most difficult to weed out. But if your decision is made and you continue to strive, to pick yourself up after each defeat and start again, then your ultimate success is assured.

This chapter on the power of thought is in three parts and is condensed from Rosicrucian teaching that normally takes three years. Much of it parallels current psychological teaching but it is essential that it be included here in order that you may have a clear understanding of your inner processes before proceeding further. It is quite true that you might succeed in employing the power of thought without a good comprehension of all the facts—the laws of chance permit this—but the Rosicrucians do not believe in blind attempts of a hit-or-miss nature. They prefer to know. And I want you to *know*.

There are certain simple exercises which you can employ to help you gain emotional control. Here are three that I recommend to you. Perform each once or more every day until you feel confident that your emotional nature is responding to your mind in a more docile fashion than at present.

1. Take a box of ordinary blue-tip kitchen matches and spill them all out on a table. Mix them thoroughly and then place them all back in the box with all of the tips pointing in the same direction. Pointless? Not exactly. A very excellent, though quite simple, exercise. Do it once a day.

2. Sit in a room with the television set turned on with normal room volume, but do not look at the picture. Turn your head in the other direction, if you must, but do not look at the picture—not even a quick look. When you have succeeded in "not looking" then try not to hear or understand what is being said and done. This is more difficult. If you do not have a TV set, do the same exercise with a radio by directing your attention away from the sound. This also is difficult. As a warm-up exercise you might reverse the process and shut out all awareness except the radio program. This is easier. When you succeed, turn to a musical program and try to shut out awareness of all sound except that of one musical instrument. If you can follow a violin or a clarinet through a three-minute interval you are then ready to go ahead with the first part of this exercise. Do this as often as convenient but at least once each day until you have mastered it. This may not seem like a training in emotional control but, believe me, it includes all the basics.

You have probably observed that these and the other exercises I have suggested have one thing in common. They all require effort on your part. This is true. You learn about energy and how to employ the power of the mind by the simple process of making the effort to do so. In this world you never get something for nothing. Everything has its price. In this case if you make the effort, the result is assured.

The third exercise you can do every day at any place and almost at any time. It is different from the other two in that it involves your relation with other people. Here it is:

3. I want you to deliberately slow yourself down in relation to other people. When you walk in the street let others pass ahead of you instead of pushing ahead of them. If you drive a car, drive it at a speed less than the legal limit. When you

encounter another car on the road, give it the right of way. When entering or leaving a room, a plane, a train or an office, let those near you precede you. Do this all with a pleasant smile and a cheerful friendly attitude. This is a great exercise. If you practice it daily for just a month you will be a new person.

Before we go on to part three, there is one more human function you should understand. The physical and emotional natures interact upon each other, as you know. An emotional disturbance either stimulates or inhibits the normal functioning of the physical equipment. In the same manner, you are very likely to feel emotionally depressed when your vitality is at low ebb. But this reciprocal effect occasionally results in odd manifestations. A Rosicrucian student made the following report on just such a reaction:

> When I was a young man I at one time courted a well-known and very beautiful actress. It was my practice to meet her after her performance each night and since she never ate very much before going on stage, she was usually hungry when I picked her up at 11:30 P.M. So we would go to a restaurant or night club and she would have a hearty meal. Even though I was seldom hungry at that time, I would usually eat something to keep her company.
> She was a fine girl, but like any beautiful young woman she was proud of her appearance and took pleasure in the power her beauty gave her over men. She was pressured by many admirers and would recount her adventures with this or that one while busily eating a steak or a large portion of roast beef. She knew this made me jealous and I guess she enjoyed seeing me squirm, little realizing that she was also giving me indigestion from which I suffered far more physically that I did from the mild and fleeting feeling of jealousy.
> Within a year or so she went to California on a moving-picture contract and I never saw her again, but the effects of those midnight snacks are still with me. At first I didn't understand. I knew I had a predisposition toward indigestion and had to be very careful what I ate. But it was not until some ten years later that I finally understood that I also

had built into myself a more serious reaction. I often became jealous, unreasonably jealous, and it was only after one such experience where there was obviously no cause for jealousy that I tried to analyze what was taking place within me. Only then did it dawn on me. I had eaten a rather poor combination of food and as a result was suffering an attack of indigestion. This physical disturbance in some way touched off the reciprocal emotional reaction which many years before had caused indigestion, jealousy. It became clear to me then that many times when I had unreasonably and falsely accused others of doing things to make me jealous, the real culprit had been in my stomach, the pressures and pains of indigestion.

The foregoing report initiated a survey which disclosed that physical circumstances and physical conditions frequently stimulate emotional reactions which seem unreasonable and are certainly not predictable unless you are aware of the pattern which was initially stamped into the individual consciousness. Only you yourself can successfully search out the initiating cause, but when this is found and understood, the physically stimulated emotional reaction can be controlled and eventually eliminated. Many human problems stem from just such patterns stamped upon the consciousness, sometimes at an early age. Modern psychiatry is now aware of this and seeks to aid people free themselves from them. The key words here are "free themselves." No good psychiatrist or analyst will claim such ability. Their best and most successful efforts are directed toward helping the patient see and understand so that he may himself re-establish normal stability.

The same is true for you in your work to unlock the power of thought. You must make the effort. You must ferret out and eliminate the physical and emotional habits and inhibitions that detour your thoughts into ineffective channels. It is you who must establish a pure line of thought.

We have thus far discussed physical-etheric energy and emotional energy. In the next chapter you will be told how to manipulate and control mental energy.

SIX

The Power of Thought: Controlling Mental and Psychic Energy

For those who would learn to employ the power of the mind the injunction is given, "Seek, find and follow a pure line of thought." The Hindu scriptures call this one-pointed thought. As you are aware the word "pure" is here used not as the opposite of "unclean." It has no reference to morals or sin, but the sense of "uncluttered thought." A great teacher has said, "Achievement is impeded primarily not so much by doubt as by inchoate thoughts generated by old habits." The desire for mental power should be as an arrow fitted to a bow. It must be launched with a mighty effort and the aim at the desired target must be perfect. But even after a successful launching it may sometimes be deflected by unexpected obstacles. Thought is the arrow and every thought is potentially creative. Select the best targets, and may your arrows reach their marks.

When man came into being on this planet he found he was in an environment that supplied all his needs. Some of the South Sea Islands exemplify this. The climate was mild, the air clear, the sun warm. No clothes were required and there was an abundance of fresh water and food to be had just by picking it from a tree. This ideal environment is symbolized for us in the Bible story of the Garden of Eden. Man had all he needed. No work was necessary and his every wish appeared to be granted even before he expressed it. This was—and is—a product of the thought of a Great Being.

But man is also a thinker. Man possesses the unique ability to create by thought. So eventually certain more advanced men discovered they could change this environment and change it they did, but not always for the best. These first "improvements" were extremely simple but from modest beginnings, which probably extended over a million years, grew the desire of man to "better himself" and his surroundings. At first his endeavors were only physical and to the present day this is the area that commands most attention. But now there are some who see the need not only to improve their environment but also their reaction to this environment. It is with these relatively few struggling souls that man's best future lies.

Dimly recalling past glory, man tries to command the elements, to bend them to his will, but only partly succeeds. Sometimes even his successes are failures in the larger sense in that they result in distortions and ugliness. Much of what man has created has little real value and some is even harmful. Only a scattered few over the centuries have actually sought to create evil but many men have blindly brought into being creations that destroyed themselves and hurt others. This is symbolized in the story of Frankenstein. Nearly everyone wants good for himself and for others, yet in their blindness many forge evil. They seek what they imagine to be "good" but through selfishness, or fear or pride they strike out at and hurt others. This is the worst sin, to hurt another, and it is the reason why all esoteric and religious teachings tell us, "Seek to heal, not hurt."

This is mentioned at the very beginning of the instruction on the use of mental power in order that you may understand and be warned that selfish use of mental power can be dangerous to others and is always dangerous to one's self. This is not meant to imply you should not use your mind to obtain certain material benefits. On the contrary, this is exactly what mental power is designed for, the control of one's environment. But there is a right and a wrong way and the wrong way is to advance yourself at the expense or damage to another. Actually it is easier to create new things, new wealth, than to compete with others for something that already exists. There is so much richness available to you, waiting just to be tapped by your mind, that it is wasteful of your energy to struggle for an area of wealth already claimed or sought for by another. If you *must* have what someone else desires or already possesses there is something wrong with your own emotional structure which I seriously urge you to repair.

Learning True Thought Control

As the first step in learning thought control you should examine the thinking process and try to understand what takes place. This is possible because we have all built into us a unique ability —we can think and we can also examine ourselves and our thinking process while we are thinking. Actually we are thinking all the time, certainly every waking moment, but we do not often notice it. We take it for granted, much as we do our breathing and digestive processes. Thoughts flow continuously through our minds and these thoughts by their very nature are creative. They make us what we are and they create our environment, the world about us, the things that happen to us. For everything we see, everything we hear, everything that we become aware of through any of our senses first existed as a thought in the mind of a thinking being.

This statement is not easy to prove. Like many others which are not immediately evident, proof of their truth lies mainly in the doing. For example, an accomplished pianist may say that Tchaikowsky's First Piano Concerto is more difficult to play than a Chopin Waltz and the average person will accept this statement because he has no way of determining whether it is so or not. Only by learning and playing both compositions can one prove it out for one's self. Most of us will accept the musician's word. He is the expert. In the same way we accept the statement of an advanced Being that thought is all pervasive and all creative as far as our world is concerned.

A student once asked his teacher about this. He wanted to know why a physical world was necessary if thought is all-creative and all-pervasive. He didn't ask the question in just that way, but phrased it as you may have put it more than once. He asked, "Why was I born? Why do I exist as a physical being?" His teacher, who was a Great Sage, replied, "In order that you may be trained to think properly," and proceeded to explain. In the thought world there is no perceptible time interval between the initiating thought and the creation of the thought form. To human awareness they are simultaneous. For this reason all untrained and poorly disciplined beings, such as we humans are, find it impossible to distinguish between cause and effect in the mental world. But in the physical world, where all vibrations are much slower, there is always a perceptible time lag between the initiating thought and the physical manifestation. Sometimes, as in the case of human action, the interval may be short, seconds only, but as a rule it is much longer. When a change in the established physical world is required it may take ten days, months or even years. This time lag gives our slow observation the opportunity to detect and distinguish between cause and effect. This is why we live in the physical.

The interval between mental cause and physical effect can be observed by everyone, but the connection or relation between the two is not always evident. Thus part of your training is to seek out causes. Do not take things for granted, for everything has a cause, sometimes immediate, sometimes remote. Start with obvious relationships, such as that when you put your finger in a flame the heat will cause pain, or when you put a towel in a pail of water it will come out wet. Then move on to more subtle connections such as the causes of a riot. Here we may find that because the night was too hot for staying indoors there were many people on the street with nothing to do; also the prolonged heat spell had made them all irritable; third, there had been a man haranguing them about how unfortunate they were and how many injustices had been heaped upon them; and way down near the bottom in importance on the list of causes there is the actual incident that precipitated the riot.

You can and should seek out and analyze three or four incidents in the newspaper each day. You won't always be right in your assessment of causes because your information may be incomplete or the news story written with a bias. But it will give you the necessary training. Much more difficult is to discover the causes of your own actions. We always like to appear in a good light to ourselves and this leads us to conceal (from ourselves) the true causes of many of the things we do. Whenever we inwardly regard a cause as unworthy of the image we have of ourselves we bury it deep in the subconscious and give ourselves some superficial but more acceptable reason for our behavior. If you persevere in your study of yourself—and you should—you probably won't like what you find. No one does. But the discoveries you make and the adjustments you apply will make you a better person, a happier person and a more successful person.

Thought Radiation

Now, let us proceed with our study of thought. Each thought at its inception produces a dual effect. *First,* there is a vibratory wave, a radiation from the center, not unlike the radiation of a radio wave from a broadcasting tower. This wave moves outward equally in all directions with gradually diminishing intensity which varies with the distance. It continues to emanate from the mind of the thinker as long as the thought is held but it ceases instantly the thinking changes or stops. Like all other vibrations, these mentally induced vibrations tend to reproduce themselves whenever the opportunity presents itself. You are familiar with the experiment in physics in which a tuning fork is made to vibrate by striking its corresponding note on the piano. In this same manner do these mental vibrations provoke in another mental body their own rate of motion. In other words they tend to arouse in a receiving mind thoughts of the same type as those in the mind of the originating thinker. The distance to which such thought waves penetrate and their impact upon the minds of others depend upon the strength and clarity of the original thought.

It is not unlike speech. Sound waves are created by the voice and radiate in all directions. The distance to which the voice will penetrate depends upon the power and clearness of the original enunciation. Also, hearing will not always mean understanding. In the same way many thought vibrations impinge upon minds which fail to register them because they have no way to relate them to their current knowledge. Attention is also a factor. A man struggling to solve a business problem is not likely to register even the best mental message on an unrelated subject. But in general a forceful thought will radiate farther than a weak and undecided one, and clear, well-defined thoughts penetrate better than those which are vague and confused.

Generally these thought radiations convey more the quality of the thought than its details. For example, if a highly developed and dedicated person were to enter a room full of people the waves of thought and feeling which pour out from him would affect everyone present. But the response would not be the same in every case. Each would have his devotion and ideals stirred in a way most familiar to himself and this would probably be different for everyone. The one thing in common would be the general raising of the vibratory nature. Everyone who thinks high thoughts pours out the kind of vibrations that tend to stimulate a similar level of thought in others. They act vigorously upon minds accustomed to high thought but also affect to some degree every mind within the sphere of their radiation. This tends to awaken duller minds to higher possibilities and to stimulate those not ordinarily given to spiritual ideas, so that everyone who thinks on a high plane is doing a form of missionary work even though he may not be aware of it.

Thought Forms

The *second* of the two effects of thought is the creation of a form. As has been pointed out, we move in a sea of energy which is most responsive to thought. Every impulse sent out from the mind clothes itself immediately in a vehicle of this vitalized matter. Thus, the thought becomes for a time, long or short, a quasi-living creature with the thought force acting as its soul and the vivified essence acting as its body. These strange forms exist on emotional as well as mental levels and some writers refer to them as "elementals." If the thought is about someone else, the thought form (or elemental) moves to that other person and discharges its qualified energy upon his mental body. If the thought be about one's self, as the vast majority of the average person's thoughts are, then it hovers about ready to react upon its creator whenever he is in a relaxed or passive state.

For example, a man fond of food may think about a sumptuous banquet topped off by rich desserts. While at work and concentrating on his job he may forget all about this even though the thought forms he created are hanging over him like a cloud. But when he leaves his office and his attention is no longer concentrated on his work, the craving for food will strike him. He may think to himself that this is merely his appetite returning, but in this land of plenty one almost never has time between meals to develop real hunger. In his case the desire for food is but the reaction upon him of his own thought forms. This would be equally true of a person who harbored impure thoughts and of course it is true in a myriad of other ways. When the attention is otherwise engaged, the thought forms are held aside, submerged below the level of awareness, but as soon as the mind relaxes they return and fill the conscious mind. A person with a religious background might describe this as being tempted by the devil, but actually it is but his own thought creations that return and demand his attention and indulgence.

Each person travels through life enclosed in a veritable cage of forms which he has created by his thoughts and desires. Through this opaque medium he looks out at the world and quite naturally everything he sees is colored and modified by the vibratory screen he has built. This is what is meant by St. Paul's statement, "We see but through a glass darkly." Until he achieves good control of thought and emotion he lives in a world of illusion where nothing is ever quite the way it seems to him. In addition to the influence it exerts on our actions, every thought form has a tendency to reproduce itself in the physical world as an action, an event or a physical thing. A very weak and tenuous thought form will disintegrate long before this "out picturing" can take place. But one powerfully endowed will usually result in a physical manifestation in a relatively short time. The word "usually" is used here because there are many millions of thought forms being

created every minute of the day and often certain ones are dia-
metrically opposed to others. In this case they effectively cancel
each other out. It is fortunate for us that they do, for mankind
does not as a rule create good thought forms. It has been said
that when even the smallest thought enters without opposition
into the megaphone of space, it attracts to itself many locusts of
the same kind, thus causing the smoky atmosphere of the planet.
One can imagine the millions of low-grade thoughts moving like
dark swarms of locusts over the face of the world and creating
around it a murky and smoky atmosphere.

Students frequently say, "I don't see how this affects me. I
don't see any murky atmosphere. The sun seems to shine brightly
during the day and the stars are clear at night." It is difficult to
grasp the concrete reality of thought. We are taught and trained
in such a way that only the audible word is given importance.
In our educational systems there is no serious attempt made to
study the power of thought. The feeble efforts of J. B. Rhine at
Duke University and others like him have not been accorded
scientific standing and it will probably take some major move,
such as interest by the government of a major power, before any
really large-scale and productive research is undertaken. Therefore, surrounded by incredulity as we are, it is not surprising that
we fail to apply this knowledge to our everyday lives. Thoughts
are silent and invisible to most and this creates the illusion they
are ineffective and not important. But we should choose our
thoughts as carefully as we choose our words and not allow them
to ramble aimlessly, creating we know not what kind of future
for ourselves and others.

Every Thought Tends to Reproduce Itself in Physical Form

For emphasis let me repeat that every thought has a tendency
to reproduce itself in physical form. Some thoughts are too weak,
some too complicated to ever reach the physical stage, but a clear
thought repeated again and again is almost certain to create a
replica of itself sooner or later. Sometimes there is a long interval,
but a clear non-competitive thought, well visualized and repeated
often, will always manifest physically.

Let me tell you a true story which will make this clear. There was a young man who was out of work and needed a job badly. He heard of the power of thought and tried to employ it to create a position for himself in the business world. He had no idea what kind of opportunity would present itself and, since he didn't want to block out any possibilities, he confined his visualization to a picture of himself sitting in a private office, his office, just four walls, a window and a small desk, but as the days and weeks went on and he continued this visualization faithfully every day, he kept adding to the picture. Gradually it grew larger. Pictures appeared on the wall, the desk became one of carved wood instead of the simple metal one he had first conceived. As the office grew larger his own ideas about it expanded and he thought, "Why not a closet where I could keep an extra suit in case I should have to stay in town for the evening?"

Then, having gone that far, he thought of a dressing room and bath in a little annex to the office. He visualized bookshelves on the wall behind him and a large picture window off to his right. Thus his visualization changed and expanded. He kept faithfully at his daily meditation and never despaired as the weeks went by. Eventually little details started to creep into the picture, details which he had not intended to put there. For example, although he was in New York and expected to work there, he could see a palm tree swaying outside the window. It was about this time he got a job, a good job, with a simple office of just four walls and a metal desk. It was nothing like the picture he had seen toward the last, but it was a job and he was satisfied, so he gave up the visualization.

But now comes a sequel. Fourteen years later, having become quite successful, he bought a home in Florida. It had a large living room with picture windows in it and one day as he sat there before a carved desk which had come with the house he idly gazed out of the window to his right and suddenly a recollection struck him. It was the palm tree swaying outside the window that did it. This room in which he sat was a replica of the room he had visualized many years before. True, he had thought of it then as an office, not a living room, but the bookcases were there at his back, there was a dressing room and bath directly off it and a palm tree swaying in the breeze outside. I can vouch for the accuracy of this down to the last detail because the man involved is myself.

Bringing a Thought into Physical Manifestation

The most important factor in bringing a thought into physical manifestation is the clarity of the visualization that accompanies it. This will be treated in detail in the chapter on "Prayer." I must now assume you have been performing the training exercises given and others like them which you have designed for yourself. After a few weeks of this discipline you should begin to understand how to use your mind. To continue the simile of a child learning to use its muscles, you will have passed the toddling stage and are ready to acquire some more sophisticated mental skills. Directions and exercises will be given you starting with the next chapter but right here I would like to pass on to you some practical suggestions which are offered by an advanced student.

1. Avoid chaotic thinking and try to think logically. People who think chaotically are like those who wave their hands in the dark, unaware of the objetcs they hit. Since we cannot avoid thinking we should at least learn to think in an orderly manner. We are ourselves living thought and it is extremely difficult to control the incessant stream of material, the substance of our consciousness, which flows from our minds into space. If we could we would indeed be supermen. But let us do what we can. As soon as we are aware of the negative thought, push it out. Replace aimless thoughts with precise ones. Actually they are less tiring. Each person, being different from every other person, should devise his own special pathway of logical thought.
2. Avoid untruthful or distorted thinking. How many secrets of bad luck can be explained by distorted thinking! Observe, as far as you are able, the consequences of untruthful or distorted thought, sometimes called prejudice. Cease jeopardizing your own future. Stop releasing dark, dangerous thoughts, for these come back to you like a boomerang in

the form of "bad luck." Here is much traveling dynamite that should be investigated both personally and also on a national scale. Of course, it is not easy to think straight. Most people are so crippled by their unconscious thoughts and prejudices they don't know if they are thinking truthfully or not and when things go wrong they are not aware of the connection.

3. In addition to correction and counterbalance, adopt a positive attitude. A benediction sent into the world is the purest and finest form of thought energy. Your own projects can grow by benediction. Unfortunately people are usually so beset by personal problems this seldom occurs to them. Their desires for advancement, better social position and the approval of others dominate their thinking in a confused fashion. To ignore these tendencies is impossible, to try to rid one's self of them is futile. The best course is to try to steer them into better and higher courses. It is a question of direction. The same exterior influences may move you to the same old course of action but when your aim is toward a higher objective your action becomes a move in the right direction. No one becomes perfect overnight and this does not mean you will no longer make mistakes. But as you become aware of the laws of energy and begin to handle the tools of thought with greater competence you will find your whole life changing for the better. You will become happier, better adjusted and more at peace with yourself and others as your power over your environment grows. And it surely will if *you* sincerely and faithfully follow the directions herein given.

SEVEN

Healing Through the Power of Psychic Energy

In Chapter One we touched briefly upon the need for balance in the human system and I gave you two exercises designed to achieve and maintain this balance. Now we will explore much more completely the whole concept of Rosicrucian healing and other useful exercises and treatments will be described.

In his book *"Man, the Unknown,"* Dr. Alexis Carrel wrote:

> Those who investigate the phenomena of life are as if lost in an inextricable jungle in the midst of a magic forest whose countless trees unceasingly change their place and shape. These investigators are crushed by a mass of facts which they can describe but are incapable of defining in algebraic equations.

Dr. Carrel, one of the world's greatest biologists, was apologizing for the vast majority of his colleagues and attempting to explain why they were still stumbling along trying to ameliorate effects rather than correct causes.

Another profound thinker commenting on the problem of human ills said, "Nowhere in human thought is the darkness greater than in connection with the laws concerning disease and death." Our best minds are groping toward an understanding of these laws and achieving a certain measure of success, yet their present position is still one of relative ignorance. As Dr. John

Erdmann, then chief surgeon of New York City's Post Graduate Hospital (now the University Hospital) once said ruefully, "There is so much we don't know."

The chief cause of illness lies in the fact that the average person continually and repeatedly abuses his body. It is amazing, all things considered, that we are as well as we are. Our automatic repair equipment is so efficient we often repeat a serious and damaging abuse for years before we are finally forced to face the consequences in the form of a physical breakdown. Sometimes the cause is easily detected, sometimes it eludes the best analysis. Whole volumes can be written on this subject but the most I can hope to do in this treatise is to correct a few popular misconceptions, to lay the groundwork for a better understanding of the healing process itself and teach you what you may do to heal yourself and others.

There are three basic ways in which a healing can be brought about. All three have their place and value.

First, there is the generally accepted treatment by a doctor. Under this general heading are grouped the allopathic and homeopathic schools of medical doctors, radiation and heat-treatment practitioners and those of the various osteopathic and chiropractic disciplines. All have done and are doing much good and constructive work and our debt to the wisdom, skill and unselfish attentions of these physicians is great. They deal all the time with urgent conditions, because almost no one goes to a doctor until he is pretty sick or needs help badly. Actually they are frequently treating dangerous effects of causes which are not apparent on the surface and of which they know little or nothing. In the face of these handicaps, their success has been little short of miraculous. They have their place in the healing picture and you should not hesitate to consult them when need arises. But remember, when you do that you are placing yourself in the hands of an outside party in whom you should have confidence and in giving that confidence you should therefore be passive, quiescent and receptive.

Second, there is that group of physicians and trained psychologists who recognize that many physical ills stem from mental repression, confusion and disorder and attempt to deal with these subjective conditions. They seek out the wrong attitudes of mind, the psychoses, inhibitions and complexes which bring about disease in the body and precipitate neurotic and mental disasters Under the methods of this group the patient is taught to cooperate with psychologist or analyst so that he may arrive at a proper understanding of himself and learn to eradicate those inner compelling urges which are responsible for unpleasant outer results. These physicians have taken a large step in the right direction and have done remarkable work. Unfortunately their work is not so simple as some of them may think. The human psyche has many subtleties only a few of which appear on the surface and this leads often to overemphasis of the observed to the consequent neglect of other factors much more important in the thought and emotional world of the patient. Thus I urge you to be extremely cautious in placing yourself in the hands of a psychologist or a psychoanalyst. To consult a medical doctor is often good because in his hands you are, or should be, passive and negative. But the essence of modern psychotherapy lies in seeking out and obtaining the cooperation of the patient. You are taught to be positive and active and it is extremely unwise for a person like yourself, whose psychic centers are beginning to open, to expose yourself to this kind of treatment at the hands of anyone but the best, in other words a genuine intuitive practitioner. It is normally better to avoid second-party interference in what is after all a voyage of self-exploration. For the one who can help and guide you right, there are twenty or more who will send you off on pointless and sometimes dangerous quests. There is enough information and guidance in this book to enable you to understand yourself if you but try. Use it.

The Best Healer—the Golden Elixir

Third, there is the employment of psychic energy. This is the energy that creates and supports life. It is also the best healer, the golden elixir. When present in sufficient supply it vitalizes form with its potency and eliminates those congestions and obstructions which are such a fruitful source of disease. It can be said that all disease is the result of, or exists because of, an insufficient supply of psychic energy. The true art of healing consists, therefore, in so releasing psychic energy that it flows through all of the organs and parts which constitute any physical form. These words sound simple enough but the processes involved are far from simple. They require that you learn certain controls which can be acquired only by practice. But they are controls which anyone can learn to employ and which you may already be using to a certain degree. Let me explain.

There are many causes of pain and death. These range all the way from environing conditions for which you are in no way responsible, such as accidents, or attacks by animals or other men, right on through all sorts of troubles for which you are partly or entirely responsible. These include infections, diseases due to early malnutrition or hereditary causes and range on to those physical, emotional and mental breakdowns which can be directly traced to your own actions and weaknesses. All of these conditions as they manifest in the physical body are in themselves results. If you can find the cause and change it, you will get a different and hopefully a better result. But even if you cannot find the cause you can alleviate and often eliminate the result by bringing in psychic energy. I will describe first how to heal yourself and then how to heal another.

To heal yourself is much more difficult than it is to heal another. Many very successful healers, well known for their remarkable cures, have almost no success with themselves on those rare occasions when illness strikes them. But this need not be so. The important element is to start work at healing yourself before the distress incapacitates you. No one can heal himself or anyone else if he is delirious, or has high fever or is so weakened he is unable to think clearly. Never let your energy charge get low and you will always be able to cure yourself so long as you can control your thoughts.

The first step in self-healing should be taken by you right now, today, before there is anything wrong with you. You should take steps to increase your store of energy and maintain it at a high level. This in itself will protect you against most infections and other illnesses. And it will give you a solid foundation from which to start a conscious healing process should accident or sudden illness strike you down.

How to Greatly Increase Your Healing Energy

Most people take their energy, or lack of it, for granted. They are aware that some people have more energy than others but aside from an occasional twinge of envy, seldom give it a thought. It never occurs to them to wonder why this should be or if there is something they can do to correct it. Yet you, or anyone, can greatly increase the amount of energy you normally have available for use. There are many techniques. Here is one such exercise, quite simple, which takes about two and one-half minutes.

1. Sit erect but not tense—or stand easily with your weight evenly balanced between both feet.
2. Take a deep breath to the count of five.
3. Slowly relax and let the air out for the count of ten.
4. Repeat this ten times consecutively.
5. While performing this exercise close your jaws firmly and clench each hand into a fist. Keep all of the body relaxed except the hands and jaw. As you breathe in and out think to yourself that each breath is bringing a great surge of energy and power which you are storing within you.

A quite noticeable stimulation will be apparent to you within 15 or 20 minutes after completing this exercise. What is not so evident is a general increase in total energy which will persist for several hours. Only beneficial effects will be observed and the exercise can be performed several times each day, four or five times if convenient. By practicing it at least once a day from today onward you will gradually increase your energy supply and in a month's time you will be so strengthened that most infections and diseases will pass you by.

Another very practical and stimulating exercise is what is often referred to as "A Child of the Sun." It involves a visualization and its effectiveness will be in direct ratio to the skill employed in visualizing.

1. Sit erect and relaxed with feet touching and hands clasped in your lap.
2. Visualize the sun, a great white flaming orb of prodigious energy.
3. Mentally lift your consciousness from your body and go "in spirit" to the sun. Enter into its flaming aura and proceed to the body of the sun itself.
4. Have no fear. You are a son of the Sun and this is your rightful home. Let the sun's tremendous energy flow through your entire being invigorating and strengthening every particle.
5. After one minute return to your body, rise and go on with your daily tasks.

Immediate stimulation and refreshment will be noticed but the greater benefit from this exercise will not be apparent for several hours. It is then you will realize, if you are observant, that you have done more work with less fatigue than is normally possible.

While taking steps to increase your energy, it will be wise if you also try to correct damaging habits of eating, drinking or thinking. Each person is different and it has been said that "what is one man's meat is another man's poison." It is impossible therefore to give you recommendations as to diet. You yourself must learn to observe from your own reactions what is beneficial and what is causing harm. Most people are creatures of habit and custom. They drink what their neighbors drink and they eat what is on the menu or what is put before them. This is not wisdom. Seek out your own best course and then have the courage to follow it. The dividends in health and well-being are great.

A certain amount of daily exercise is also important. I do not suggest that you become a health faddist. All extremes are bad. But your blood must be kept circulating and a walk or some other mild exercise each day is the best way to stimulate it. Nor should it be necessary to mention cleanliness and the importance of a daily bath. Thus your health is safeguarded.

All Ailments and Disorders Can Be Remedied

There may come a time, however, when due to accident or to circumstances beyond your control your good health is attacked. Whether it be disease or muscular pain or nervous disorder makes no difference. All can be remedied and cured if approached soon enough. The key is thought and the ability to visualize. Here is a way to cope with most such situations.

1. Sit (preferably) in a comfortable chair. Hold your head erect and your spine straight. Separate your feet and allow your hands to rest in your lap unclasped.
2. Visualize yourself surrounded by a white cloud, a very bright, scintillating white light like sunlight upon new-fallen snow.
3. Then see that white light becoming more and more concentrated in the painful area.
4. If the trouble is in the heart or lungs, visualize the concentration of light in the region of the fifth and seventh thoracic vertebrae of your spine. This is between and slightly below the shoulder blades. The sympathetic nervous system controls most of the automatic bodily functions. Supplying extra energy to the proper point of the sympathetic nervous system where it parallels the spine stimulates the system to increase its repair activity and thus speed up the return to normal of the ailing or damaged area.
5. For nervous disorder (not mental aberration) concentrate the white light in the neighborhood of the fifth cervical vertebrae. This will bring relief and strength to a depleted nervous system.

If you are in such pain or distress that your power of visualization is impaired, the foregoing treatment may be difficult. In such cases, seek the aid of another who can give you the proper treatment or have recourse to a call to your higher self, as described in the chapter on Prayer.

How to Heal Others

To heal another is usually much easier than to heal one's self. The best method is to gather energy and supply it to the patient. This sounds simple but there are many methods and all need explaining. Before beginning, though, let me remind you that unless you are a licensed physician you are specifically forbidden by the laws of most states to make diagnosis and prescribe treatments, or to suggest, recommend or prescribe internal remedies of any sort. Remember this. These laws are right and good and for your protection against charlatans and fakirs. However, the Rosicrucian healing treatments given here do not transgress any laws because they are applied in a super-physical manner somewhat like prayer. Just remember not to offer a diagnosis to the patient. Never say to him, "You have this—or that—the matter with you." Keep what you think to yourself. You have been asked to heal, or help in some similar way, so confine yourself to giving the proper treatment in the most effective manner.

Before attempting to heal another let us first consider yourself, the healer.

(a) It is important that you be in good health. This is not always necessary but in the vast majority of cases it is a "must" for success.

(b) You must have purity of motive. This does not mean you must be entirely pure in heart. If only the pure of heart could act as healers we would have very few healers. But there must be purity of motive, in other words your sole objective must be to help the afflicted one in every way you can. You must not be "showing off," for example. This "purity" is essential in order to provide an unimpaired passage for the flow of psychic energy through your own vehicles before it is released into the patient. The ideal in so-called "magnetic purity" is reached when the two major head centers which correspond to the pineal and pituitary glands are linked and functioning together. This is achieved through meditation and purity of life. Not many have achieved this ideal but fortunately a lesser measure of efficiency is possible without this perfectly functioning equipment and for most of us this is the best that can be expected.

(c) It is valuable if the healer can get some inner understanding of the nature of the patient's disease or ailment. This often is possible to attain by establishing a certain degree of attunement. When the inner stages of thought, desire and feeling of the patient can be observed by the healer, he can pinpoint the cause of the trouble and direct the psychic energy unerringly to it. This ideal method of treatment is well beyond average ability, but there are many who have trained themselves for it. When using it, be sure you are well aware of what you are about, because even a partial attunement with a sick patient may result in the unprepared healer's picking up some of the symptoms of the patient. Properly energized you will not suffer the ailment itself, but you could have some uncomfortable moments. Usually such attunement, while helpful, is not necessary. Any intelligent patient can describe with fair accuracy what is bothering him and you in turn can take proper steps to cure him.

(d) Before starting a healing treatment, be sure to build up a reservoir of psychic energy within yourself. This is done by visualization, as is most esoteric work, but it must be accompanied by the attraction of desire for the energy and by will as a conditioning and directing agent. You must *visualize* psychic energy pouring into you and actually feel its power. You must *want* the energy to accumulate for the unselfish purpose you have in mind—the healing of another—and you must seek to make tangible conscious contact with this energy in order to properly manipulate it. Then take three deep breaths, holding each to the count of seven and then releasing them slowly. While taking these breaths, bring the first two fingers and thumb of each hand together and hold them in contact, each hand separate from the other. You are then ready to begin your treatment.

Let me say here that the Rosicrucian healing treatments are in no sense miraculous. For the most part they just speed up the normal healing process by supplying more energy to the right places and thus aid the human system in its work of repair. Suggestion can and sometimes does play a part. But in many cases the patient cannot or will not accept suggestion. It is most difficult for a person suffering excruciating pain from arthritis, for example, to accept a suggestion that he is perfectly well. So the Rosicrucian treatments do not rely on suggestion, although this technique should not be ignored where it can bring about good results. Generally the Rosicrucian method is to apply extra energy, psychic energy, to the spots where it will do the most good.

Now let us consider the patient. On the subject of the patient and the innumerable ailments he might be subject to, whole volumes can be written. It is not easy to condense into a few pages a veritable encyclopaedia. Therefore I can here make no attempt to consider the cause of the patient's ailment, although this is important, or the nature of his disease, which is even more important, if you are to act with intelligence and the greatest efficiency. For the present, you will just assume the patient is ailing from an unknown cause and has asked for your help.

(a) If he is able and willing to cooperate, ask him to relax and calm his mind and emotions as much as possible. Suggest that he think of a quiet pool of clear water in a deep forest. Not a ripple disturbs it and the white clouds overhead are perfectly mirrored in its depths as they sail majestically along through the bright blue sky. Tell him what you are doing and why as you go from one step to the next. In this way the power of suggestion will be added to your efforts.

(b) Having calmed the patient and placed him in a receptive mood, repeat your own accumulation of energy. Accompany your deep breaths by visualizing the psychic energy flowing into your body from above and accumulating there in the region of your heart. The energy must be contained there by an act of your will until you are ready to release it into the patient. When you do not have a definite knowledge of the ailment, as in the present imaginary case, you should transmit the energy into the heart center of the patient. This is done by directing it into his back adjacent to and on the left side of his spine between the shoulder blades. This can be done in two ways.

(c) *By contact.* Place the index finger, the middle finger and thumb of your right hand all touching each other on a spot on the left side of the patient's spine between the shoulder blades. Then release the accumulated energy into the body of the patient through the heart center with which you are making physical contact. It is important to have the proper visualization at this point. You are not releasing a limited amount of accumulated energy such as pouring out a container which eventually empties itself. You are instead opening a valve into an unlimited supply of energy which will continue to flow through you into the patient as long as your visualization is clear. The original accumulation by you is more in the nature of a pump priming. The continuing flow is far greater than your personal containment. Normally, you can with practice maintain a clear visualization for thirty to forty seconds. When it clouds or changes, remove your hand, relax and wait about five minutes. Then repeat the entire procedure starting with your own breathing and accumulation of energy. Usually three such treatments at one time repeated again in their entirety at two- or three-hour intervals will show results in twelve hours and frequently a cure in twenty-four.

WARNING: Never touch a patient unless he or she specifically requests a contact treatment. Then only touch lightly with the finger tips as directed with no massage or rubbing.

(d) *By radiation.* This method involves no physical contact. It usually works better if you are in the same room with the patient and can see him. This gives you the opportunity to visually direct the energy to the spot you select. However, it can be employed at a distance. The hands are not considered and the entire process is carried through by the use of the mind, will and heart.

It is important in both the foregoing techniques to observe the following very closely. While the psychic energy is being collected, being evoked so to speak, the will is used but the moment you turn your attention to the patient, the will must become quiescent and the force of love must take over from that point onward. In other words, the act of healing is an act of love. If the love force is strongly felt it can be most successful in bringing relief and cure to the patient, and at the same time a dividend in the form of increased vitality is paid to the healer himself. Remember this, and if you find your energy depleted after giving a treatment, or if you have taken on some of the symptoms of the patient, you will know you have erred in some basic step. Examine in retrospect what you have done and endeavor thus to discover where you went astray. In most cases where this occurs the point of error lies in failing to make sure that love, a great, openhearted, generous, dynamic love, takes over the first moment your attention turns from yourself to your patient. This shuts out all fear and doubt, the focal point of infection.

In discussing this treatment certain students have asked, "Am I disturbing or disrupting the karma of the patient by healing him?" The answer is, "No." There are many vaguenesses and inaccuracies in our conception of karma, and the inevitability of cause and effect is one of them. Actually it is not the set affair which modern thought surmises but is related to the laws of thought far more closely than is suspected. We do not always have to pay a like penalty for a rash action or a stupid mistake.

Those who originally spoke to us of karma tried to make clear a very complex law and as a result oversimplified it. They made the laws of karma and of retribution look like one and the same. Actually, the law of retribution is only one aspect of the law of karma and the Old Testament ruling of "an eye for an eye and a tooth for a tooth" does not always hold. You should give help and energy whenever it is called for and wherever you can. Never withhold your giving because you fear it may not be karmically right. Who are you to judge? And even if you were correct in your judgment, how are you to know when the moment for mercy comes?

Learn how to heal. Practice until you become proficient and give generously where you can. Healing can be administered in many quiet ways. Riding in a plane recently we encountered bumpy weather and were tossed about. A baby in its mother's arms became frightened and started to cry. This was partly because of its attunement with the mother and caused partly by the sensation of falling, of the withdrawal of support which is one of the instinctive fears of all babies. It was not difficult to enter its consciousness and convey to it a feeling of warmth and security. Its fears gone, it ceased crying and was asleep within a minute or two. This is a form of healing which can be practiced any time, any place. The object does not have to be an infant. A Rosicrucian reported recently that while he was traveling in a suburban train late at night, a man, visibly intoxicated, became disagreeable and started to annoy a stranger who sat near him. It looked very much as if there would be violence, since both men were large and strong. At this point the Rosicrucian student sent an aura of love to the aggressor. Almost at once his attitude changed from his previous angry belligerence. He started to chuckle and after making one or two silly remarks, curled up at the window and fell asleep.

Cuts, Wounds and Abrasions Heal More Rapidly

There are many aspects to psychic healing but the foregoing techniques are basic. Psychic energy is the energy of human life. If an individual has an abundance he is free from all annoying illness and infections. When you supply extra energy to another, you help him free himself. Also, cuts, wounds and abrasions heal more rapidly where the psychic energy is in plentiful supply. Even animals can be helped in this way. For example an advanced student of Rosicrucian principles reported the following:

> One day as I was walking in the country with my dog, an Irish setter, he flushed a rabbit and chased it into the brush.

In his excitement he ran into a dead bush and one of the branches broke off in his eye. It was horrible to look at, with the end of the broken branch sticking out of his eye and few drops of blood running from it. Calling him to me, I took his head in my lap and with a quick jerk removed the sharp branch. The wound was large and gaping but I held him quiet and gave him several positive treatments, directing the energy into the spine directly back of the head and at the same time visualizing it flowing into the eye and healing it.

After about ten minutes I lifted his head and looked at the eye. The bleeding had stopped and the wound was much smaller. I could see then quite plainly that the hole was in the lower portion of the eyeball beneath the pupil. With him on leash to keep him quiet, we started for home, nearly an hour's walk. He appeared in no distress and trotted quietly beside me. When we reached the house another look showed the wound down to almost a pinpoint, and the following morning there was no trace, not even a scar.

Relieving a Headache with Directed Flow of Psychic Energy

Sometimes a normally energetic person will have the life-giving psychic fluids blocked off from a certain area in his body, with resulting distress. This usually has an emotional cause, which should be sought out and eliminated. However, you can relieve the tension and cure the ailment by supplying psychic energy directly to the affected part. For example, a headache can be relieved by placing the tips of the first two fingers of your right hand on the left temple of the sufferer and the index and middle finger of the left hand lightly against the right temple. Then visualize a flow of psychic energy going from the fingers of the right hand into the head and out on the other side through the fingers of the left hand. After three or four minutes the pain will disappear and, if the cause is removed, will not return. Always wash your hands both before and after giving this treatment and, of course, all contact treatments of any type.

If a person has a cold, or is showing the nervous and irritable symptoms that usually presage an oncoming cold or virus infection, a negative treatment as described in Chapter One is best. In this case you are bringing the psychic energy down to the physical level and applying it in the manner best suited to cure the ailment. The term "negative" is purely relative and in no way implies negativity in the sense of passive or non-active energy. In these situations, you, the healer, act as a transformer. You gather the psychic energy, step it down to the etheric level and then deliver it through love to the patient.

Easing Aches and Pains by Delivering Energy to Area of Irritation

Pains and aches can be eased and often eliminated by giving positive treatment, in other words by delivering energy to the area of irritation. It must be remembered though that if physical deterioration has proceeded too far, psychic energy treatments will not succeed. For example, if tooth decay has reached the root and an abcess has been formed, it is far simpler and better to either remove the tooth or sterilize the root canal.

Likewise broken bones should be set by a competent bone specialist and it is better for torn ligaments to be properly re-fastened than to just grow them together. This can be done, but the more efficient method is by surgery. This can and should be supplemented with Rosicrucian healing treatments. There are on record literally thousands of cases where the subsequent recovery was unusually fast and without complications. To give an example of how this works, here is an actual case history.

Place:	Hospital of the University of Pennsylvania 34th & Spruce Streets, Philadelphia, Pa. 19106
Date:	March 11, 1967
Problem:	Female patient had a vaginal hysterectomy performed and after being returned to her room it was discovered that clear water was flowing from the vaginal tract but with very little urine coming from the normal opening. The attending surgeon made a cystoscopic examination and discovered no bladder leakage—a dye had

previously been instilled into the bladder. However, further examination disclosed that the left ureter had been clipped at the time of the operation. The patient's bladder, kidneys and ureter all appeared to be of healthy tissue, so the surgeon decided to wait ten days to see if natural healing would take place before attempting surgical repair.

Treatment: It was at this point that the patient petitioned help and Rosicrucian absent (radiation) treatments were started. Within twelve hours time the abnormal drainage had stopped and an examination disclosed that she was completely healed. The surgeon in attendance expressed his amazement and said he had never before seen such a rapid systemic correction, the normal time for natural repair being several days and more often than not, surgical repair is required.

This chapter would not be complete without comment upon the dissipation of energy. You have been told how to accumulate and increase your energy. You should also know how to conserve it. We all waste energy. If we only consumed energy by work we would all be completely healthy and would actually be capable of many times the amount of work we presently do. But we dissipate our precious energy in a thousand ways all unwise and most of them unnecessary. Here are a few big energy-consumers to avoid—worry, fear, resentment and hurry. Each chews up large quantities of energy and I dare say you allow one or more to plague you each day. Don't. You are the boss. Don't let these emotional parasites prey upon you. Remember, everything you turn your attention to is the recipient of some of your energy. You literally give it away. Sometimes you get part or all of it back, as when you admire and rejoice in the beauty of a flower or a sunset. Sometimes when you unselfishly care for another your dividends are greater than the energy you use. But far more often you dissipate it unnecessarily through your eyes and other senses. You look here or there sometimes out of curiosity and sometimes just because your attention is captured or demanded, and each time you give away something of yourself. Your eyes dissipate a great deal of energy. A realization of this by teachers of old led them to instruct their pupils to fasten their gaze upon the tip of their nose when attempting to meditate. This has no value except to reduce the dissipation of the pupil's energy and to help him keep his mind upon the seed thought. Of course, in our present living conditions it is impossible not to look. Usually our very lives depend upon this form of alertness. But when you have been made aware of the potential energy waste you can reduce it enormously. Think about this. You can make yourself a much more powerful person just by effecting an economy in this one department.

Now in the next chapter I will discuss the law of cycles and tell you how you can use this law to benefit your life, your health and your fortunes.

EIGHT

Understanding the Law of Cycles

People often ask if the Rosicrucian Order teaches astrology or numerology and when they are told it does not, seem surprised. "I thought the Rosicrucians were modern mystics," one man said, "and does not the study of both astrology and numerology belong in the arcanum of mysticism?"

The Rosicrucians are modern mystics, but very practical ones. Their training is designed to guide the sincere seeker to become a master of his destiny as symbolized in the Tarot by the card entitled "The Magus." This card portrays a man with confident bearing standing upon the bank of a river or sea. Flowers grow at his feet and fish swim in the water. But his head is held high among the stars. The symbolism is clear. This is a man with both feet planted firmly on the ground. His foundations are secure and one knows he will make no misstep. Yet his attention is not focused upon the earth and the waters below. The flowers wave in the breeze and give off their scent and little waves break at his feet, yet his gaze is heavenward and his thoughts are with the stars. This is the Magus, the ideal human being toward which we all strive either consciously or without realizing it. This is the archetype to be attained through study and practice of the Rosicrucian teachings.

Significant it is that this Magus has his feet upon the ground. So has the ideal Rosicrucian. He is aware of the arts of astrology and numerology but does not lean upon them. Not because they are false, for they are real enough, but because they are incomplete. Both embrace too many unknowns. The Rosicrucian instead makes a thorough study of the cycles of life and thus is able to substitute practical certainty for mere possibility. Let me explain.

Everything Is Subject to Cyclic Law

Everything you can see, hear or touch, everything you can be aware of in any way, is subject to cyclic law. This means it vibrates at, or responds to or is moved in a certain definite rhythm. The earth revolves on its axis every twenty-four hours, creating day and night. It travels around the sun every 365¼ days and this results in the rhythmic changing of seasons. Mountains are raised sharp and clear against the sky. But as wind and rain and sunlight take their toll, the peaks become rounded hills and after thousands of years return once again to rolling plains. Trees from small seeds grow large, then wither and die, each in its own time. Everything in the universe and, indeed, the universe itself, lives and moves in cycles.

No one knows why this is so, but everyone knows that it *is* so. We are born, grow up, learn, work, play, love, reproduce and then grow old and die. We human beings have our cycles, but unlike the earth and the plants and the stars, we can control to a large degree the what and when of our existence. We need not be slaves to the things of fate. We have free will!

There are those who will dispute this. They say we are forced by circumstance to make what seem to be free choices but what are really conditioned reflex actions and are thus determined for us in advance. This is only partly true. There are many decisions from which we cannot escape, but on the other hand we *know* there are many occasions each day when we are fully capable of taking either road presented. This is not illusion or self-deception. Looking back on a choice made and observing that it was not to our best advantage, we can, without the slightest restraint, proceed to follow a course directly opposite. This does not deny that man is constantly subjected to tendencies, urges, impulses, inspirations and propitious presentations in the form of opportunities and temptations to good, evil and neutral acts. The same may be said of Cosmic influences which affect human beings in the form of tendencies, but there is no power that *forces* their acceptance upon man. He is ever a free agent to choose between one impulse and another, one inspiration and another or one temptation and another, but having chosen, he must accept the responsibility for his decision.

Even though we accept the fact that man is a free agent with the power of free choice, it is still necessary to consider the nature and source of the impulses, urges and temptations that come before him and call for him to make a choice. If these diverse opportunities did not present themselves and if these varying impulses and urges were not occurring each moment, there would be no reason for him to have free choice. Nor would he have occasion to reason or to think or to use his will.

Of all living things, man alone is unique in the possession of the ability to act freely, but unfortunately the majority usually choose unwisely and the salvation and advancement of the human race has been left to a relatively small minority of dedicated, clear-thinking, farsighted men and women. You can and should be among these leaders. So start now to live in harmony with the law of cycles as I will explain it. Then you will find yourself going through life "with the wind at your back," as the Irish so colorfully put it.

Work in Harmony with the Cosmic Rhythms of Your Nature

We are all daily faced with the need for recognized decisions. The man in his business, the woman in the home, the child in school find themselves face to face with perplexing problems which could have serious effects on their future. As these people decide, so they will determine their fate and establish their destiny. But to yield to an inspiration or an impulse or temptation with no other warrant than a judgment based upon analytical reasoning is in most cases like gambling on the toss of a coin. It is impossible for human reason to go beyond the knowledge and information in the mind of the reasoner, so that even in those rare cases when the reasoning is clear-cut and perfect, the decision may still be wrong because the information was incomplete. However, there are periods or cycles in everyone's life when an urge followed will act toward a successful conclusion whether that action be a business proposition, a journey, the building of a home, the buying and selling of merchandise, or anything that is created or brought into existence by natural law or the will of man. By working in harmony with the proper periods the utmost success can be attained, but if one persists in working against them, it is like swimming upstream and usually ends in defeat. You are a free agent. You can work in harmony with the rhythms of your nature or against them. You can thus become master of your fate or a slave to circumstance. Choose!

Many people try to ignore the unusual in life because they do not understand or cannot learn the logical theory which explains it. It is not too difficult to argue against the possibility of a cosmic rhythm which affects your actions and welfare. One can make quite a case. But do not be too quick to accept mere reason. You may not be in possession of all the facts. You know the story of the ranch hand who encountered for the first time an electrically charged fence. He had seen wire fences all his life. He had built many corrals out of wire and he felt he knew all there was to know about wire fences. But one day he came to one of those modern corrals lightly constructed of only a double wire strand. Naturally he was contemptuous because he couldn't see how it would hold a two-day-old calf, much less a full-grown steer or horse. The owner warned him not to touch the wire because it was charged. The ranch hand didn't know what this meant and to show his contempt he reached to tear it from a post.

Well, you know what happened. The shock knocked him down and scared the wits out of him. Then at last he began to see why the animals in the corral were careful to keep from touching the wire and to realize that things are not always so simple as they appear to be. So try not to be too much like the cowpuncher.

All the energy in the universe has a single Source. Some call it the Cosmic, some the First Cause, some call it God. Whatever this Source may be, we don't know much about it. We may reason about it but even the most highly illumined sages do not pretend to know or understand it. When this energy reaches our level we can begin to comprehend it; the broader and higher our development, the better our understanding. The wise men in all ages and among all people describe it in much the same way. The ancient Chinese pictured it as a trilogy, the opposites yan and yin which when united form the Cosmic circle. The Christian theologians refer to the three Persons in God and the Rosicrucians to the three sides of the Triangle. The Hindu seers were more explicit. They said the primary energy divided first into three different energies and then into seven. The ancient Kabala of the Hebrews says the same but in a different way in its description of the ten Sephiroth, again, three and seven. Everything in the universe received its primary impulse for existence from one or another of these Seven but was also subjected to the influence of the millions and millions of ramifications, subtle and gross, of the energies supplied by all seven.

The early experimenters in rocket propulsion were frustrated by the apparent inefficiency of this presumably ideal method. They had failed to apply a basic truth and tried to propel their vehicles with a continuous flow of burning fuel, like a skyrocket. What they overlooked is that there is no such thing as continuous pressure in our universe. When they came to the realization that everything is moved by a repeated impulse they incorporated that idea into their engine design and succeeded. Our present-day jet planes and rocket moon flights are the result.

The law that is true on the human level is also true on the highest level we can imagine. The Great Sephiroth or the Great Ray (call it what you will) that energized you at your birth continues to support you with impulses that are characteristic of Its own unique quality. Any thought or action of yours that is initiated while this impulsing energy is gaining momentum carries along quite easily toward success, while those begun in a descending cycle are almost always doomed to frustration or failure. You can prove this law yourself by means of a simple experiment. Throw a ball forward while running forward. Note how far it goes. Then throw it forward again with the same energy while standing still or moving backward. See the difference? Once this law was discovered, the Rosicrucians studied it with great interest, but the problem facing them was to learn how to apply it, and this took centuries of study. Now, today, the fruits of those years of effort are available to all. Detailed instruction in the application of cyclic law is part of the Rosicrucian teaching and available only to Rosicrucian students, but the basic principles can be revealed and will be explained to you in this chapter.

The Cycle of Existence

Everything in the world, whether created by nature or by man has a cycle of existence distinctly its own. This refers not only to men and mountains, to machines and vegetables, but also to corporations and diseases and even ideas and emotions. All have a definite starting point and a distinctive pulsation, or rhythm of existence. These cycles are like lines drawn out for various lengths and divided throughout their length and duration into equal segments.

The line of your life can be compared to the line the captain of a ship marks on a chart for the course he intends to follow. An ocean liner going from New York to Gibraltar may take seven days, so the captain will mark on the line the position he expects the boat to be at the end of each day. But not every day will be the same. The start may be foggy and cold, the next day rough and windy, the third day warmer but with headwinds that slow the boat, the fourth day bright and sunny and so on. So it can be said that the pulsation or periodicity of the journey is seven days each with its own characteristic influences. The journey of life is much like such a sea voyage. Each life begins at a certain time and place and is divided into periods like the days of the ocean journey. The average person is not aware of these periods which present opportunities or obstacles at different times, and is therefore not prepared to meet them until they are in full manifestation. He is then handicapped in resolving them properly by his lack of knowledge of the assisting or hindering tendencies which exist in that period. Not only your life itself but every enterprise you enter into has cycles which begin at its inception. Thus the information which follows is of value not only to you personally but may be applied to your business, or to any business or organization or project in which you may take interest.

Medical science and the students of biology and physiology agree that human life is divided into a progression of periods of seven years each. From birth to the age of seven there is a period of self-discovery in which the growing child learns his relation to the material world and begins to adjust himself to it. From seven to fourteen physical growth and muscular control are important and although the mind expands, it is a secondary consideration. Toward the end of this period the distinction between the sexes shows itself. The third period is one of mental as well as physical growth and the fourth, one of growing spiritual awareness. The fifth is a creative period and so on. Human beings were designed by the Creator to live for twenty-and-one-half periods of seven years each, or about a hundred-forty-four years. Of course, today no one lives that long. In fact half, or seventy-two years, is usually considered a good long life and those who live longer are regarded as exceptional. This shortening of the potential life span is the result of man's failure to live according to the laws of nature, but our knowledge and self-discipline are increasing and human life is gradually lengthening.

Most cycles have seven divisions like the seven days of the week or the seven notes in a musical "octave." There is a reason for this which has to do with the origin of energy itself, but here we have limited space and can consider only the effects and not their cause. There are also cycles of three, four and twelve periods, but those of seven are the most frequent.

Your Private, Yearly Life Cycle

Just as a human life is divided into periods of seven years, so each year in that life is made up of seven periods. Starting with your birthday there are seven periods of approximately fifty-two days and each one of these periods provides you with different possibilities, opportunities to be seized or problems to be solved. The calendar year has nothing to do with this cycle. This is your private cycle and it extends from the day of your birthday in one year to the day before your birthday the next. To work properly with your own yearly cycle, get a calendar and, starting with your birthday, count off fifty-two days. Thus if you were born on January 5, circle the date and also circle February 26, which is the fifty-second day. This is your first period. Make a chart of this for the entire year so that you can always tell at a glance in what period you are. When you have done this, write or type the following and keep it so that you can always have easy access to it.

Life Cycle, *First Period*
(Date_____ to Date_____)

This is the period of opportunity. It is the best time to advance your interests with others who may have the power and influence to help you. This is the time to ask favors, to seek employment or loans or business concessions, to form partnerships or to make investments. This is also a good time to advance yourself among the people of your city, state or country, to build up your credit standing or your reputation. This is the best time for you to push yourself forward with determination so far as your name, your integrity and your honor are concerned.

Life Cycle, *Second Period*
(Date_____ to Date_____)

The second period is distinctly different. It is the best time to plan short journeys or trips of immediate importance. It is also an excellent time for moving about, if that should be necessary. In other words this is a period propitious for changes that can be started and finished within the period itself. In a business way it is a good period for movable things such as freight, cargoes, automobiles, trains, public conveyances, or even public lectures or performances which may move from place to place. It also presents excellent opportunities for those who deal with liquids, milk, water, chemicals, gasoline, oil and other products of this character. Dealing with people who are in businesses associated with the foregoing will be more successful at this time than at any other. This is also a very good period for businesses which cater to transients such as hotels, restaurants, car rentals and similar services. However, one should not plan a change of business or start a new career or make any permanent change during this period, and contracts and other arrangements that are intended to last a long time should not be entered into. It is an unfavorable period to borrow or lend money and it is not good for starting the construction of a building or entering upon a project that requires a substantial investment. Certainly it is a most unfavorable period to speculate in the stock market or to gamble in any form.

Life Cycle, *Third Period*
(Date_____ to Date_____)

This period requires that you exercise discrimination and good judgment. It usually brings a great inflow of energy which makes you want to do great and important things. If directed carefully this can be the best time in the year to improve your health or build up your business or do anything that requires the expenditure of energy. However, good judgment is needed. You will be tempted to undertake projects which have no possibility of success or which may take so long to develop that you will have to abandon them before completion. But this is a great time to tackle and overcome obstacles that have blocked progress in the past, to make a strong second effort to solve problems earlier abandoned because of lack of energy. It is a great time for dealing with things that require great energy such as iron and steel, electrical machinery, cutlery, sharp instruments and fire. It is also a particularly good period to oppose competitors or deal with enemies who have heretofore been obstacles in your path. It is an unfavorable period for men *or women* to try to deal with women but on the other hand it is an excellent period for women to appeal to men when desiring favors or preferment or aid in business or social matters. Arguments and strife should be avoided because the outcome is very apt to be bad, but if you have something to sell which can be put across in one forceful interview, this is the best period.

Life Cycle, *Fourth Period*
(Date_____ to Date_____)

In this period the mental and spiritual nature is stimulated. It is thus an excellent period for writing books, producing plays, making plans, for all matters requiring imagination and quick thinking and the ability to express your
thoughts lucidly. Your mind will be filled with new ideas
which will come very rapidly, so it is important that you
grasp them quickly and put them into practice before they
are forgotten or pushed aside by the new thoughts which
will crowd upon their heels. It is therefore a good period to
act on impulse or hunches. You will be optimistic in this
period but somewhat nervous and restless, which is to be
expected with your imagination highly charged. It is a good
period to deal with literary people, writers, journalists,
book or magazine publishers, but be careful to scrutinize all
legal and other documents most carefully because deception
is possible and it is a period when falsehood is as eloquently
and easily expressed as the truth. Most great losses through
robbery or deception or misunderstood legal situations occur
in this period and you should take precautions to protect
yourself. However, it is a good time for study and for gaining
information and knowledge, but it is not a propitious period
to enter marriage, to hire help or to buy homes, businesses
or land.

Life Cycle, *Fifth Period*
(Date_____ to Date_____)

This is the period in which it is possible for you to achieve
your greatest success in your personal affairs. This is the time
in your yearly cycle when your interests will expand and your
prosperity increase. Your mind likewise will become a more
effective instrument, sharper and clearer, you will become
more open in your relations with others, move with more
confidence and display sociability, benevolence and sympathy.
This is the best period for dealing with the law, with lawyers,
and judges, the courts, government officials, men of promi-
nence in the profession and people of wealth. It is also a good

period to begin new ventures that may take some time to grow, to plan large business negotiations or to undertake long journeys. It is particularly good for collecting money due or for speculations in stock or real estate, but be sure to avoid every negotiation that is not completely legitimate. Also avoid any dealings in cattle or meat products or with marine affairs.

Life Cycle, *Sixth Period*
(Date_____ to Date_____)

This is the best time in your yearly cycle for rest, relaxation and amusement. This does not mean that business will not prosper. On the contrary, all good and legitimate business will continue with almost as much success as in the preceding period. However, now is the time to make long or short trips for the purpose of renewing friendships or for cultivating new friends, men among women and women among men, and to renew and improve friendships and relations that already exist. It is a particularly fortunate time for business matters that touch upon art, music, literature, sculpture, perfumes, flowers and personal adornments. It is a good period for a man to seek preferment or favors or business agreement or cooperation from a woman, just as the third period is better for women to obtain such favors from men. It is the best period to buy stocks or bonds for investment and to employ others.

Life Cycle, *Seventh Period*
(Date_____ to Date_____)

This is the most critical period of your yearly cycle. During these fifty-two days the elements in your life that are no longer needed for your development gradually fall away in order to make way for those which are new and better. Often this will cause distress and a sense of loss and may tempt you to foolish actions and decisions. Remember it is a period of seeming devolution which always precedes a period of evolution and new opportunity. Take advantage of the momentum in this period to rid yourself of the old and unwanted, but be sure to exercise good judgment. If there is something that has been hanging fire and is about to end, let it do so, but do not deliberately break ties or destroy relationships that have vitality and are still valuable. For the reasons mentioned, your mind is likely to become despondent and you will be easily discouraged. Remember you are being influenced by the quality of the period you are in and do not permit the pessimism you feel to warp your judgment or inhibit your decisions. The qualities of this period exert very subtle influences and it is necessary that you be much more alert than normal in appraising your feelings and your reactions to external influences. In the Fourth Period it is advisable to seize immediately upon your ideas or hunches and make quick decisions. Now the reverse is true. Impulsiveness will bring disaster. Be careful in all necessary judgments and postpone to the next period every decision possible. However, this is a good period for dealing with older people and those who by their nature or position must consider each action most carefully. It is also an excellent time for inventing things or dealing in inventions or for applying for patents or copyrights. Now you will have success in dealing in real estate, mines, minerals and all things deeply seated in the earth or in hidden places. On the other hand, it is definitely the least favorable time of your year to start anything new or launch a new business or to make new expenditures in an old one.

To a certain degree the influences of each period will overlap the one before and after it. Thus it is advisable to be careful in all judgments and actions on the last two and the first two days of each period.

If you would like to make a quick check on the reliability of the foregoing information, find the dates of your seventh period and check back over what occurred between these dates each year for the last ten or fifteen years. I am sure you will discover that your worst frustrations, disappointments and "bad luck" happened then. Try it.

Your life cycle is divided into seven-year periods and we call this your major cycle, or cycle number one. Each year likewise is divided into seven periods, each of fifty-two days, and this is called cycle number two. We are assigning numbers to the cycles because there are a great many. We will treat with only two more, the business cycle, which we will call cycle three, and the health cycle, which we will call cycle four. This is all we have space to describe and, in fact, all that the average person normally cares to study. However, the Rosicrucians have made a thorough study of cycles and have experimented with them over many hundreds of years and they willingly teach their students all they know. These additional cycles take the influence of the moon into consideration and cover the long lunar cycle of twenty-eight days and how it breaks down into three and one-half day periods, each with its own quality and influence. Then there is the short lunar cycle of twelve hours, which in turn breaks down into four three-hour periods. Each period, short and long, exerts positive and negative influences of certain types which affect us, our lives, our business affairs, plants, the tides, fish, animals, sex, mental attitudes and in fact, everything. This study is about as involved as that of business bookkeeping, but a good student can become proficient in about six months. He can then describe with accuracy all of the aiding or hindering influences which are present at each hour of the day, week or month, and recommend the best course of action.

The Business Cycle

Everything has its own cycle of existence, marked off by periods of definite duration. This cycle starts on the day when the person or object or plan or association or business comes into existence. It is important, therefore, when considering the cycle of a business, that you know the day the business started. With an incorporated business this normally would be the day on which the articles of incorporation or charter were granted. A partnership would date its inception from the day the agreement was signed. However, there are many businesses where the starting date is not so obvious. Do not make the mistake of assuming that the tax year or the fiscal year starts the same day as the company did. It might or it might not. If there is no documented starting date, try to discover the day the business opened its doors, or when the doctor or lawyer or accountant hung out his shingle. Consider this then the beginning of the cyclic year and calculate accordingly.

In the case of a business that has changed hands or changed its name, the date on which the firm began to operate under the new name or with the new owners would then be the birthday of the business, regardless of how long it had been operating before that day. In some cases the day on which a group of people might gather together and decide to start a business and actually assign control and duties to certain individuals would be the birthday, and not the day on which the announcement was made to the public. As you can see, this point may require some thought and study.

Business Cycle, First Period
　　(Date＿＿＿＿ to Date＿＿＿＿)

Begin by marking the birthday of the business on a calendar and then checking off the dates, fifty-two days apart, that measure the seven periods. During the first fifty-two days of each yearly business cycle the business will find great success in promotion and advertising. It is an excellent time to build up sales and good will. This is the time to solicit endorsements from authorities or prominent people and concerns that will result in favorable publicity and eventual sales increases. Contracts with government officials will go smoothly and efforts to obtain favorable legislation or protective bills will receive thoughtful consideration. The direct aims of the business in this period should be to enhance its name, reputation and prestige.

Business Cycle, Second Period
　　(Date＿＿＿＿ to Date＿＿＿＿)

During the second period of its yearly cycle a business will find the best time to make changes in employees and their duties, temporary changes in location, modifications of business practice, or tentatively to try out new plans and propositions. On the other hand, it is not a good time to enter into new agreements, to make any long-term plans or to enter into contracts of any kind unless they are reduced to writing. Verbal agreements made are very likely to be ignored or changed at a later date. However, it is a good period to build up business friendships and to contact prospective customers or clients.

Business Cycle, Third Period
(Date_____ to Date_____)

This is the best building period and the time when all growth factors should be pushed to the utmost. It is also a propitious time to collect and get money. However, it would be wise to avoid the courts or legal contention with business enemies, although other legal matters having to do with positive growth and expansion will meet with favorable reaction and should be pushed. Watch out for accidents, disasters, troubles from competitors and enemies, or sudden explosions of wrath, enmity or hatred within the company and also outside, but affecting it. Manufacturing plants should guard against fires or explosions and all businesses should be on guard against enemies who may attack their life and reputation. If the business deals with the army, navy or any military department of the government, negotiations will go very smoothly in this period.

Business Cycle, Fourth Period
(Date_____ to Date_____)

This is the time to initiate the largest advertising campaign. Promotion to customers and the public will have greater success now than at any other time of the cyclic year. It is also a good time to make new agreements and draw up new contracts, transfers and similar documents. Now is the best time in the business year to deal with newspapers and newspapermen, with diplomats and negotiators. However, care must be taken lest deceptions be made or tricky agree-ments offered, for these could cause trouble later on.

Business Cycle, Fifth Period
(Date_____ to Date_____)

This is an excellent period for growth, expansion and financial success, to seek out and make investments, to obtain credit or extend time in which payments are to be made. It is about the best period for selling and for delivering merchandise sold, from which good profits will result. It is a good time to collect long-standing accounts and even debts considered bad and an excellent time for getting a favorable decision in the courts if right is on your side. It is now the best time to expand to foreign lands or to deal with interna-tional concerns and it is a particularly good period to pro-mote relations and business affairs with railway and elec-tronic companies and with all companies that cater to the happiness and pleasure of the public.

Business Cycle, Sixth Period
(Date_____ to Date_____)

If it is necessary to relax business activities at any time during the year, this is the time to do it. This is the best period for the chief executives and managers to take vaca-tions and it will be found that the affairs of the business will continue to prosper in their absence. However, if your busi-ness has to do with the production or sale of music, poetry, art objects, artists' materials, high-fashion women's clothes, articles of adornment, beauty preparations, high-priced auto-mobiles, oriental rugs, antique furniture or any other luxury items, by all means keep at work, because this is the best time in the year for you. This is also the best time in the year for the heads of the business, or its owner, to establish personal friendships with its customers in order to help the business in the future. It is also an excellent period for collecting money, buying stocks and bonds or promoting the finances of the company through sound investments and it is also a good time to form partnerships, combines, subsidiary corpora-tions and alliances aimed at ultimate expansion.

Business Cycle, Seventh Period
(Date_____ to Date_____)

This is essentially a reconstruction period and must be treated as such. Do not start any new activity, do not go heavily into advertising or expansion of a new line or new department. A certain tearing-down must be expected and all new plans should be held up until it is over. Likewise, if you foresee changes that will necessitate the elimination of departments or personnel or the abandonment of certain factory sites in favor of better ones, this is the period in which it should be done. But great care must be taken lest the destructive wave carry too far. This tendency is powerful during the seventh period and could affect aspects of the business which should be protected, so be on your guard. No new alliances or contracts should be made and all actions should tend toward the conservative. Great diplomacy and care must be applied at all times both in contacts within the business and with others on the outside, whether they be customers or suppliers or city or federal officials. Nothing of a radical nature should be permitted in selling or advertising or buying or, in fact, in any department of the business during the seventh period. Caution and conservatism should govern every action.

A business which follows these guide lines has a far better chance to succeed than one which moves ahead in a haphazard fashion. In fact, some of the largest and best known and most successful corporations in the United States already use these patterns. You can do the same. Remember, though, that you, yourself, will have two cycles to deal with, your own personal life cycle and the cycle of the business in which you interest yourself. Of course if your birthday and the birthday of the business should coincide you have no problem. But when they do not there will be overlapping and conflicts. In these cases you must exercise judgment. When the influences oppose they must be blended, so analyze them carefully before you act. Here are certain points that may help you. If the business is entirely your own you may be guided by the conditions governing your personal life cycle, because these will be more influential than those governing your business. However, the business itself must be carefully watched and any tendency to follow an unfavorable cyclic trend must be corrected immediately. This is another case where "forewarned is forearmed." If you know what might happen and are alert to its possibility you can take counter measures in time to prevent a serious problem arising.

If the business is not your own but a corporation or a business belonging to others in which you are only a small invester or an employee, then the cycle of the business will control and must be followed even though it may conflict at times with your own. Remember, there are many times in the affairs of successful men when personal preferences, needs and desires must be set aside in order that the business may prosper. The important point is whether your own affairs are so related to your business that they will both suffer together or prosper together, or whether they can be separated so that the business may prosper while you are having difficulty and vice versa. Here your importance to the business must be a consideration. If you are but a minor employee and your acts are restricted to obeying rules and carrying out orders, then your personal cycle should be followed. On the other hand, if you hold a position of trust or of vital importance and the future success of the business hinges on your decisions, then you must consider the business first.

The Health Cycle

Health Cycle, Period One
(Date_____ to Date_____)

Make a chart similar to the one for your personal life cycle. Start it on your birthday and mark it off in fifty-two day segments as before. During the first period your vitality and health should be at its best and if you happen to come into the period with your physical condition below normal, it will improve rapidly if you take care of yourself and avoid breaking any of the natural laws. Plenty of good air, walking in open and abundant water are the basics. Foods heavy in starches and those that are overheating should be avoided. The eyes in particular should be guarded. Do not use them overmuch and avoid using them in bright electric light or exposing them to direct sunlight. If an operation is needed, or a system of health building is to be adopted, this is the time to start.

Health Cycle, Period Two
(Date_____ to Date_____)

In this period a great many light and fleeting physical conditions may affect the body and passing emotional conditions may affect the mind. You may have temporary difficulty with the stomach, bowels, bloodstream and nerves, but these conditions will come quickly and last only a short time. They should not be neglected but given immediate remedial care. Then there will be no need for anxiety, for all influences present in these fifty-two days tend to bring about rapid changes in your physical condition. There are likely to be days when you will have a headache or an upset stomach, and other days when your eyes or ears will bother you, and still others when catarrh or colds and attendant aches and pains will cause distress. Women in particular may suffer pains in the breasts and abdomen. But none of these need be serious. If you are cheerful, maintain an optimistic attitude and do not let your mind dwell too much on these ailments you will find that they will respond quickly to the treatment you administer.

Health Cycle, Period Three
(Date_____ to Date_____)

Accidents may happen in this period, so be careful. If you are aware of what might possibly occur and take steps to guard against it, you will minimize the effects and may possibly prevent it entirely. There is also possibility of suffering by burns or falls or blows. Be careful of your food, too. Do not overeat and try to keep your body normally warm, because there is a tendency to take cold as a result of overheating the body. Keep your bloodstream clean and your bowels active so that you may not be plagued with eruptions in the skin and similar blood disorders. Your blood pressure has a tendency to rise in this period, so avoid overwork, overstrain and anxiety and thus protect yourself against any possible breakdown.

Health Cycle, Period Four
(Date_____ to Date_____)

This is the most trying time in the year for your nervous system. You may observe evidences in restlessness and uneasiness and also in the malfunctioning of certain organs. Too much study or reading or planning and anything which makes you tense should be avoided. If your work demands great concentration, break it up every hour or so with five minutes of light diversion. Chat with someone, listen to some music if a phonograph or radio is at hand, or just sit in quiet meditation. You require more sleep and rest at this time than in any other part of the year. If you fret and become nervous, it may affect your digestion or cause your heart to palpitate. If you observe these signs do not become worried unnecessarily, because their cause probably lies in your own nervousness. If you have been laboring for a long time at mental problems or under a mental strain, it is wise to relax and rest for a few days during this period as insurance against more serious mental difficulties.

Health Cycle, Period Five
(Date_____ to Date_____)

This is a good period during which your health should be excellent. If it is not, it can be improved quickly. Spend time out-of-doors and breathe deeply of fresh air. Observe the beauties of nature and let their healing balm reach into your physical and emotional nature. Live and eat with continence and avoid the tendency to overindulge in the appetites of the flesh, which is always very strong in the fifth period. This is a good period to recover from all sorts of chronic ailments and if you but set your mind to it, you can get rid of any abnormal or subnormal conditions which may have been plaguing your body for some time. It may be noted that your whole nature, physical, emotional and mental, will respond to mental suggestion and psychic help much more readily in this period than at any other time of the year.

Health Cycle, Period Six
(Date_____ to Date_____)

The temptation to overdue things also exists in this period. However, here it applies not only to the physical appetites but also to work, play and all excitement. Avoid overindulgence of every sort and save yourself upset conditions which may affect your skin, throat, internal generative system and kidneys. Drink plenty of water, take outdoor exercise and get all the rest you need.

Health Cycle, Period Seven
(Date_____ to Date_____)

Chronic or lingering illness may be contracted in this period, so be careful lest you expose yourself to contagions of any sort. Avoid the persons and places where they may be contacted. Since your mind and spirits may be at low ebb, take positive steps to relax and find pleasurable recreation. Adopt an optimistic mental attitude, smile at yourself in the mirror each morning and tell yourself how lucky you are to be alive and how happy and grateful you are that you have received so many wonderful natural gifts and endowments. Never mind what you really think; tell yourself that anyway. Don't dose yourself overmuch with medicine and under no circumstances have an operation performed if you can avoid it. If you give prompt attention to every upset as soon as it becomes noticeable and maintain an optimistic attitude, you will have no trouble.

The foregoing listing is for your information in order that you may know what tendencies exist and when they may strike. No one person will ever be the victim of all these ailments and troubles. In fact, if you follow the instructions in Chapter Seven, none of this will ever bother you. But you may desire to help another, and a knowledge of what may assail him at different times will aid you in supplying remedy and cure.

The most important part of this chapter is that which tells of your personal life cycle. Create this chart and print or type the opportunities and hazards that exist in each period. Some Rosicrucians make a separate card for each period so that they can examine it easily and understand better how to plan each day. They find that this gives them much more control of their destiny than heretofore and also the confidence that they are becoming like their ideal, the Magus pictured on the Tarot card.

NOTE:

The detailed description of cyclic influences compiled by the Rosicrucian Order, AMORC, may be read in "Self Mastery and Fate" by H. Spencer Lewis, Ph.D.

NINE

The Power of Prayer

There is probably no religious practice so generally accepted yet so little understood as prayer. Every person you meet will tell you he has received an answer to prayer. Regardless of caste, nationality, color or creed, all men have experienced that definite sequence of request and fulfillment described as prayer. A man prays for money and the postman brings him the needed amount; a woman prays for food and food is brought to her door. But on the other hand there is the evidence of prayers apparently unanswered, of hungry people starving to death, of the child which dies in spite of its parents most passionate appeals to God.

Any study of prayer will reveal contradictions and many facts which are strange and puzzling. A trivial prayer meets with an answer while one on an important matter fails; a simple ailment is relieved while an agonized petition to save a beloved life meets with no response. A devout person will say, "It is the will of God" and question no further, but the Rosicrucians are not content with this. As esoteric students, they realize that in prayer certain laws are at work, laws which must be discovered, identified and understood.

Let us first analyze prayer as the average person knows it. This word is used to cover various activities of the consciousness and prayers cannot be examined as if they were all the same. First we have the prayer which petitions for physical aid or material assistance. The most general definition describes it as a petition placed before a person or being who is presumed to be in a position to grant it. With this goes the assumption that the person or being can grant the petition without sacrifice or effort and with but little inconvenience to himself. Note that prayer is described as a petition to a person or a being in a position to grant it. We do not say "prayer is a petition to God," although it well may be. Since most prayers are for some physical or material aid, very few of them are actually directed to God as the First Cause. People are usually a little self-conscious in asking for material benefits and are reluctant to place such a mundane petition before the Highest One. Also much of the religious teaching over the past two thousand years has tended to make man fear God and to feel separated from Him. Thus God or the First Cause has become cold and remote to the vast majority of people, much like the president of a large corporation or the head of a great banking institution. Many feel, therefore, that their prayers cannot or will not reach God and so they direct them to some being or person who seems more accessible and who at the same time may be more understanding and tolerant of the human weakness behind the petition.

As far back as man can remember, sailors have prayed to the sea or to some entity they conceived of as the God of the Sea. They have prayed for a safe and speedy passage, a full catch of fish, or for rescue in a storm. They have also prayed to the winds and to Aeolus, the Wind God. As recently as a year or two ago in a race of sailing craft from California to Hawaii, the crew of one boat, at the time in the voyage deemed most propitious, sacrificed three chickens to the gods of the sea. These were not superstitious South Sea natives but wealthy American businessmen and sportsmen. The fact that their boat eventually won has no bearing on the point made here, which is that this act was performed in all seriousness and represented a form of prayer.

I mention this because it is a fair example of a type of petition or prayer which has always been employed by men. Sometimes a propitiatory offering is made, sometimes not. Are these prayers actually offered to some disembodied intelligence, as they seem to be? Or is this merely a device to focus attention upon the desired objective without an actual realization of the mental machinery being set in motion? Think about this.

In certain religions we find prayers being offered to holy ones or saints more often than to God Himself. Years ago an unscrupulous priesthood encouraged this human tendency because it increased their numbers, prestige and income. History tells how the priests of Egypt called for a return to the "Old Gods" after Amenhotep had proclaimed that there is but one Supreme Being. This was not only a political device to regain temporal power; it was also a direct effort to obtain more money, for by multiplying the gods, the gifts were also multiplied. Today in India and China the devout pray to Buddha, in Russia they pray to Saint Sergius, in Italy to Saint Anthony, in this country to Saint Theresa, the Little Flower; in Iran they pray to Mohammed and in all parts of the Christian world to the Holy Family, Jesus, St. Joseph and the Blessed Mother Mary. Actually there are hundreds of beings in all religions to whom petitions and prayers are daily addressed in the hope that they will recognize the justness and fairness of the request, understand and sympathize with the motives of the petitioner, and use their power or influence to help provide the material advantages asked for.

Thus we see that in the first and most common type of prayer, which is prayer for material benefit, the petitions are sometimes directed to God but far more often to some other entity or person which the petitioner believes is in a position to grant his request and may be persuaded to do so. If we probe the mind of a petitioner and ask, "Why did you pray to Saint Anthony and not directly to God?" we find that he feels that "Saint Anthony was poor once and can understand how much I need this money." And if we ask another, "Why have you prayed to the Mother Mary instead of to God?" the answer comes, "Mother Mary is a woman and she will understand what a man cannot."

As we look into the hearts of these people we realize how childish most prayers are and we begin to understand why it is that some are granted and others not. Here among the average people of the world there is no understanding of prayer. They are like children asking their parents for what they want. Sometimes they get it and sometimes not, but they never quite know why, and they seldom understand enough and have confidence enough to set out to obtain these things on their own.

Tap the Universal Storehouse of Supply

One of the primary objectives of the Rosicrucians is to teach people how to lift themselves out of this childish dependence upon others and train them to use natural law for themselves. Their students are given exercises in concentration, they are taught to focus their attention upon an object and hold it there, their memories are trained and a serious attempt is made to help them rid themselves of outworn inhibitions and erroneous ideas. They are taught that appeals for needed material things should be made to the Cosmic, the Great Storehouse of Supply, and are given the techniques which, when properly employed, are designed to tap this Universal Storehouse. These students are taught a practical method of prayer for material needs, an adult approach to the problem of supply which can be made to work most of the time once it is understood. It is not a hit-or-miss method. If the demands are unselfish, or at least not too selfish, and their granting will not hurt anyone else, they will manifest on the material plane. It is this technique which I will give you in capsule form later in this chapter.

The Petition for Light

The next level of prayer is the petition for light, for instruction to aid a man in his desire to come closer to God. This is aspiration and is almost always directed to God or to the Supreme Being. Many people pray in this way. A substantial segment of all humanity feels the yearning of aspiration at one time or another but usually at different levels of understanding. One asks for help in moral or spiritual difficulties, another for spiritual growth, a third pleads for strength to overcome temptations, a fourth for insight and so on. This is going on continuously all over the world and its chorus is referred to as the "invocative cry of humanity." It is this aspiration, this request for spiritual help which brings response from on High in the form of Hierarchical teaching and guidance. It is because this "invocative cry" is today so loud and strong that we have such a vast flow of revelation in all parts of the world. The Rosicrucian Order is one of the major channels of this flow and the thousands of students in the Order have come there because they have consciously or unconsciously raised their hearts in aspiration and petition for guidance and help.

Meditation—Attunement with the Higher Elements

The third form of prayer is called meditation. In it the student seeks attunement with the higher elements of his being and also petitions help and assistance much as in the first form of prayer, but with this essential difference—the help is almost never for himself. When he does register himself as a beneficiary, it is in order that he may gain in strength or wisdom or skill so that he may help others.

We Can Obtain from Life Anything We Want

Here, then, are the three general levels of prayer as it is understood and employed by 99 percent of the people. It is not for us to judge the quality of these prayers or whether they are good or bad. But they all have one element in common: they look to another for help. By implication, the one praying thus confesses his inability to help himself. In the opinion of the Rosicrucians this is where the error lies. We can obtain from life anything we want. It is up to us to find out how to get it and then have the persistence to keep after it until we do. Let me explain to you the Rosicrucian concept of prayer.

In order to understand a Rosicrucian prayer, a Rosicrucian mental creation, you must first realize that it is a scientific process and it will always work if all of the elements are properly provided. If it doesn't work, it means that one or more elements were missing or the process was improperly performed. A homely example is the baking of a cake. You need flour and water and milk and an egg or two and butter and flavoring to make a good cake. Even if you have all of these ingredients, you will not have a cake unless you know what to do with them and when to do it. When you have learned this and have mixed everything in the right proportions and in proper sequence, the resulting dough must be baked. Here the heat must be just right and must be applied for the suitable length of time: If it is too hot, the cake will burn. If not hot enough it will be flat and doughy. So you can see that a great deal of knowledge and skill is required in addition to good ingredients in order to make a good cake.

A Rosicrucian prayer is just as complex—and when you know how, just as simple. Not many people really learn, unfortunately. If they were sifting flour or stirring in eggs, they could learn in a short time to never overlook a step or leave out an ingredient. But when a sifting of thoughts and a baking in psychic energy is demanded, the problem in some unaccountable way seems to become much more complicated and difficult. But it is not, not really. Once you learn, it is as easy as swimming or riding a bicycle, both small miracles to one who has not yet acquired the skill. First I will tell you what you need to do to pray as a Rosicrucian, and after that I will tell you what not to do. For, strangely enough, there are many things that must be avoided.

Prayer Is Creative Visualization

Rosicrucian prayer is more often called creative visualization. We all visualize, usually many times a day. Some of us are more thorough than others. Rachmaninoff said once that he never performed on the concert stage without having played every number over in his mind the night before. He could hear every note and knew precisely where each finger should fall without either a piano or the musical score before him. This is amazingly thorough visualization requiring the utmost in concentration, and the magnificent results proved its value.

A good architect will see in his mind the completed house before he ever sets pencil to paper. Every closet, every stairwell will be placed in his visualization well in advance of the first step in preparing the blueprint. These professionals, the great musicians and the leading architects and indeed all successful planners, are very good visualizers. But for the most part, their efforts stem from a need, emotional or physical, which is present before them. The architect is given a commission, the musician has a concert planned, the businessman a product to sell. What you are to learn is the art of visualizing without a compelling need forcing you to action.

There is no secret to visualization. Everyone has this ability, but you must learn to visualize in such a way that the image you create will tend to objectify, to manifest itself as an object or an event in the physical world. For the musician and the architect this is a natural sequence—the one plays a piano concerto and and the other produces the plan of a building—but you, who may have neither piano nor drawing board nor indeed the skill to use them, must seek a different method. It is a simple technique and can be used to solve many problems. However, before putting this process into operation it is wise to understand the laws involved. First you must know exactly and quite clearly what it is that you desire to manifest. Your desire cannot cover a multitude of things, only those involved in your immediate need. When you have brought your primary objective into manifestation or physical existence, then and only then may you turn to another objective.

Nearly everyone's mind is cluttered up with rambling thoughts of no consequence. It is first necessary to clear your mind of these intruders and hold but one thought dominant, the thought of what you want. Having thus prepared yourself, you are ready to start the visualization. For this it is advisable to find a place where you will not be interrupted or distracted for about thirty minutes. The actual visualization is not intended to last that long but it may take you a while to clear your mind and bring it into some resemblance of rest.

When you have settled yourself comfortably in the place you have chosen, proceed first to relax. Start with a conscious effort to relax physically. Relax your toes, your ankles, the calves of your legs, your knees, the muscles in your thighs, relax your middle body, your fingers, your hands, your wrists, the muscles in your forearms and shoulders. Relax your neck, your face muscles and the tiny muscles around your eyes and ears and in your scalp. This will take three or four minutes and when accomplished will leave you feeling much quieter.

Now it is time to turn your attention to your mind. Since it is virtually impossible for the average person to slow down and stop the rapid flow of his thoughts, a device is now used. See in your mind's eye and with your physical eyes closed, a blank screen like a motion-picture screen. See it filling the entire space before you and visualize it as well lit up with a white light, as you have sometimes seen it between films. Now willfully, carefully and meticulously start to assemble on this screen of your consciousness a living, detailed picture of that which you wish to make manifest. Make it a living picture. See it as though it actually exists before you. This will require singleness of purpose, a good imagination and an ability to concentrate, none of which come naturally but must be acquired by practice. At first you will do very few things right, I am sure. But with practice you will become more skilful.

The Rosicrucians teach that every man and woman alive is endowed with the ability to create on the material plane. But in order to do so we must learn to use tools we have been given. The first is the ability to visualize and the second the imaginative faculty. These must work together. The imagination must provide the pictures, either from recollection or by combining parts of recollected pictures and ideas to create new ones, and then these pictures must be thrown onto the screen of our consciousness and held there. They must have duration in order to out-picture themselves in physical matter and events. The longer you can hold the exact picture without change, the more rapidly will it manifest. This is where the ability to concentrate comes in, the third point on this creative triangle. I could stop here and say, "That's all there is to it," and I would be right. You have all the basic ingredients. But you know and I know there are a lot of questions unanswered, so I will try to be more specific.

To most people the foregoing technique sounds too simple. Some don't believe it will work, and so kill all chances of success before they even start, for one of the essential ingredients is a complete and abiding confidence that what you visualize will come about. Others, seeing how simple it is, become careless and go about it in a half-hearted fashion. This is almost as if the person about to bake a cake were to put all the ingredients into a pan without properly mixing them. Some people find it difficult to visualize and others to concentrate, so you see it is not easy. But it can be done and it can be learned in a reasonably short time if you are willing to practice regularly, as you would most surely have to in order to acquire any other skill.

What You Visualize Becomes Material Fact

Now let me add some important details. If, for example, your objective is the successful closing of a business deal or the starting of a new venture, build a picture in your mind that portrays the crucial point in the transaction where the final successful act is performed. By holding this picture in your mind, clearly and strongly for two or three minutes at a time, you are literally creating that same situation in fact. Remember in a situation like the one described you are dealing with the material world, and to make changes in matter, energy is required—the greater the degree of change, the more energy needed. A simple manifestation may result from a single creative meditation. A large project may require a hundred. The laws of physics apply here just as they do everywhere in the known universe.

In creating the picture many different techniques may be employed. You may consider yourself an artist and the blank screen of your mind the canvas before you. Paint in, then, with full color the image you wish to have appear. Use your imagination and fill it in with sound and scent as well as color. If it is out of doors, feel the warmth of the sun and the cool caress of the breeze. Make it real!

End each period of visualization by turning the whole picture inward. The process is something like swallowing but you use your mind instead of your throat. Then forget it. Don't permit your thoughts to turn back to what you have done and do not permit any faint images of the picture you have painted to trail in your imagination. Put it completely out of your mind. This is essential because as long as you hold on to it mentally, you are siphoning off the energy which is necessary to its ultimate manifestation.

When you have started energy working in your behalf by repeated visualizations of your desired objective, make every physical effort possible to bring it about. Do not sit back as if to say "I defy you to manifest." Do what you can to help. Open the avenues of all possibilities. It is much easier to go through an open door than one which is closed. Remember, too, you must be convinced that what you are planning is good and desirable and that it will not hurt anyone. This is not a question of God stopping an evil deed, although at times it may seem that way, but of your own conscience short-circuiting the energy. Only an extremely evil and undeveloped person will have the ability to avoid this type of mental inhibition.

Permit me to caution you against planning recklessly. The story of the genie in the bottle who granted three wishes, all of which turned out to be foolish, is an example. Certain possibilities exist for everyone and your mental creations will be happy and successful if they keep within bounds. You may think that nothing is impossible and today this is very nearly literally true. But that does not mean that nothing is impossible to me, or to you. We both have our limitations; I have mine and you have yours. Suppose you had a sudden urge to set foot on the moon. As we know now, this is not an impossibility. But it is for me and it may be for you. So it would be foolish to consume energy in an endeavor to satisfy a futile and vain desire.

Let me give you an example of the way this law of creation can work when it is not properly applied. This is as reported by a Rosicrucian neophyte, a workman in a factory who, when he learned of this law, decided to use it to get $5,000. He persisted in this visualization daily for several months until it gradually became more and more real to him, as it does. But he took no other action and did not in any other way try to earn or obtain this money. One day while at work he slipped and fell into one of the machines in such a way that his foot was crushed. Fortunately, when he got out of the hospital he was able to walk once again by wearing a special shoe, but the whole front of his foot was gone. The company paid his hospital bill, gave him full salary while he was away from work and treated him well in every way. On the day he returned to the plant the general manager asked him to come to his office and there offered him a check for $5,000 if he would agree not to make any further claim against the company. It was then and only then this man realized how he was responsible for what had happened and where he himself had failed, and so told us the story to help others. Energy that is built up demands release, and if we do not open doors for it and guide it in the proper direction it is likely to break out in an undesirable way.

The art of mental creation here described, as its name indicates, is an act of the mind whereby energy is accumulated and directed toward a desired objective. But the Rosicrucians also teach a different kind of prayer which in some cases is much more effective. This prayer is not based on mind and will, but upon love. It works best when you pray for another. In fact, you might say it doesn't work at all for one's self. I guess this is because we already love ourselves too much, and in the wrong way. We will probably have to develop spiritually a great deal more before we can learn to pray for ourselves by loving ourselves. But we can help others by sending them love. Let me explain this.

There is an energy just as distinct and just as powerful as mental energy which for want of a better word we call "love." The warmth of the heart we feel for a loved one is the nearest sensation to the physical reaction we experience from this energy. Yet it is not sentimentality nor is it physical love, but something different and more refined. And it is a definite energy. To the astral senses it is quite tangible and pink in color, not a paint or pigment pink but the pink of light, like a glorious sunset.

This is an energy which we can consciously accumulate and then give to another. It is like food, like nourishment to his entire being and benefits the recipient in every way. Only good comes from this love. Here you need never fear an error; every giving, every sending is good. This is what Jesus Christ endeavored to explain to the people of His time. There are many techniques for employing this larger, grander love. All religions suggest one form or another, but these are usually cloaked in the atmosphere of the particular dogma of that religion. There are also many simple procedures which have no connection with any organized religion. Here is one which really works well.

This technique combines three elements, a visualization (again) a feeling and an act of the will. As in the Rosicrucian prayer given earlier, both visualization and will are necessary, as they are in almost all human efforts to control energy. But a new element is here added, that of feeling. The procedure is as follows:

1. Create a feeling of love, of warmth, of good will in your breast in the vicinity of your heart. Visualize this as a glowing pink aura which emanates from the heart and completely surrounds your body.
2. Then visualize, see clearly in your mind's eye, the person, or group, or entity you wish to help.
3. By an act of the will now send a portion of your aura in the form of a pink cloud to the object of your love. Feel love for this person or object and see the pink cloud encapsule him (or it) in a pink aura of protection.
4. Then immediately dismiss all thought of it from your mind and regard it as a "mission accomplished."

When this technique is properly performed, the results are amazing. Usually the treatment must be repeated for many days before the results are apparent, but eventually they show up in the most remarkable manner. In sending love it is important that no specific result is desired or foreseen. There must be no such planning by the sender. The manifestation must be left to the intelligence of the soul force actuating the energy and when this is done it always comes out in the most desirable manner.

Sometimes the results are on the emotional level only but always they are most practical. In a six-month test involving seven beneficiaries which was conducted two years ago, two of them received obvious emotional and psychic help but the other five got amazing physical material benefit. One woman over fifty years of age with a crippled husband and a teen-age son to support, who had worked all her life for modest wages, obtained an executive position paying over $10,000 a year. Another woman's husband was made a partner in the firm for which he worked. Two men were advanced dramatically to new positions and much larger salaries and the other three were helped emotionally to a much better understanding of life and to greater composure in the face of the daily turbulence we all have to meet. One of these three was also helped in a business way.

Unquestionably there were other benefits but these were clearly obvious. In addition, the sender was unexpectedly helped in several ways.

1. A rapport with each receiver was established and a greater understanding between the sender and each receiver resulted.

2. The sender's awareness of himself, of his own mistakes, weaknesses and glamors was heightened to a point where he was partly able to clear his own life and act with greater control of himself and his environment.

3. The sender received an inflow of what can only be described as great spiritual strength.

These are the specific benefits which were observed to accrue as a result of a daily practice of this prayer of love, a practice which involved only a modest amount of thought and effort and not more than fifteen minutes time. Feel love. Send love. Encapsule a small portion of this Kingdom of Heaven, as Jesus called it, and bestow it upon another so that it may grow like the mustard seed in the parable and bring comfort and peace to many.

Earlier in this chapter I spoke of the prayers offered by most people and described them as childish. These are the prayers that are directed to God or to some entity asking for material assistance or benefit. They are not childish because they are directed to God. On the contrary we should all look to God with a child-like faith. But they are childish in their expectation of certain material benefits and in their lack of understanding of how that help may be given.

As you realize, there are many situations in which we cannot help ourselves but can be helped by another. In fact, there would be little or no progress in this world if the enlightened few did not give their aid to the vast ignorant and helpless majority. Thus we can and should petition for aid, pray for help so to speak, whenever we feel need of it. This prayer can be directed to God or any other advanced being that we are confident can help us. And these Great Ones are ever ready to help in every way They can. To receive and employ this help is *our* problem and most of us never solve it.

To refresh your mind a bit, we live and move in a realm of energy. Our own well-being and our ability to accomplish things depends upon the amount of energy we are capable of wielding. When we ask for help from One greater than ourself and He responds, He sends energy. It is up to us to receive this energy, grasp or lay hold on it and then employ it to achieve the objective we seek. To give a homely analogy, it is just as if we wanted to buy a house costing $20,000 and we had only $200. So we go to a rich man and tell him we need the house and ask his help. He is moved to give us assistance, but does he give us the house? Of course not. He gives us money, enough to buy the house, in this case a check for $20,000. Now it is up to us to convert this check into cash and buy the house. Some are so ignorant they will say "I asked for a house and all I got was a piece of paper" and then resentfully throw the check away. Others will cash the check but then start spending the money for things such as a new car, a few parimutuel tickets and maybe several cases of whiskey. Still no house. You understand and can carry it on from there.

When we pray for help from God or some Great Being we must be prepared to receive that great energy and direct it properly to the object of our desire. First we must have a receptacle large enough to receive and retain the amount of energy we require. Then having accumulated the necessary volume, we must be careful not to dissipate it foolishly. One of the Great Teachers describes it in this way.

People talk much about the aid which they expect from Us. Let us analyze the capacity of people to accept this help. Each person who dreams of assistance has already selfishly defined the direction and measure of it. Can an elephant find room in a low cellar? But the seeker for help considers neither the proportion nor the suitability of the help

Let us examine the plight of one young man who prayed for help. This young man had a small job and it did not pay very well. He wanted more money and the better living conditions it would bring, so he prayed to his Master for help and his Master sent him a bountiful supply of energy on the returning wave. Now, this young man, like you and me, was actually looking for a new job or a windfall of money as an answer to his prayer, and he did not recognize the inflow of energy. But he felt fine and so strong that he immediately proceeded to expend a part of this energy in love affairs with several girls. These girls demanded lots of attention so he soon found himself involved in all sorts of side issues of interest to them but of no real importance to himself. One liked the theatre, another night clubs, a third wanted to attend lectures, a fourth was a pop music fan and so on. In the meantime this extra energy had given a stimulus to the young man's mind and he had several very good ideas for making money, any one of which if developed might have led to a fortune. But he was too involved with these young ladies and soon the energy he received had been so dissipated there was not enough left to carry out even one of his ideas. When his job did not miraculously change, the young man was very disappointed and blamed his Master for not having sent the help for which he had prayed so ardently. So his Master said:

Must lilies flower during wintertime or a spring burst forth from a rock in the desert in order to prove Our merit? Oh, maker of the desert and lord of the cold, you have created your own thirst and shudder from the cold of your own heart. You have encrusted your way with selfishness and find time only to guard the soles of your feet from the thorns which you yourself have planted. So my help takes flight like a startled bird and my messenger hastens back, rejected!

TEN

How to Understand and Use Telepathy

It is well to understand something about telepathy, for in years to come it will be increasingly important for you to know if and when you are responding to telepathic suggestions and even consciously to employ telepathy yourself. The very fact that you have picked up this book and have had enough interest in it to be reading this sentence is an indication you have the ability to receive and send mental telepathic messages.

There are many kinds of telepathy and mental telepathy is only one of them. Generally speaking there are three broad classifications of telepathic communication. These are:

1. The telepathy which takes place within the individual. Usually this is a form of communication between the higher self and the brain. This is stressed in the Rosicrucian teachings and is described as Cosmic Contact.
2. Telepathic communication between individuals, which we will study in this chapter.
3. Telepathy between groups or between an individual and a group.

For you as an individual, the most important area for you to develop is the interplay between your soul, mind and brain. If you can establish clear channels of communication among these three levels of your consciousness you will be on the verge of a breakthrough into Cosmic Awareness or Cosmic Consciousness.

This requires special training which I will describe in Chapter Twelve. The present chapter concerns itself with telepathic communication between individuals. Much false and misleading information is in circulation about telepathy and as a result many mistaken notions and vague ideas exist concerning it. So I will start with fundamentals.

Four types of telepathic communication between individuals are possible. These are:

1. Emotional telepathy. The connection is between the solar plexus centers of the individuals involved. It has largely to do with "feeling."
2. Between mind and mind, or mental telepathy. This is what you are to study and learn.
3. Between soul and soul, an advanced study.
4. Between any two or three of these aspects simultaneously.

Emotional, or "Instinctive" Telepathy

The most common form of telepathic communication is of course that between the solar plexus centers of two or more individuals. This is sometimes called instinctive telepathy. It occurs when emotions or "feelings" are strongly held and corresponding radiations are transmitted from the solar plexus center. When direct physical contact exists or when the auras of two or more individuals blend together, the transmission is effected quite easily. It rarely occurs at a distance, but when it does under the urge of some powerful emotional stimulus, it is transmitted on the astral level, not the mental.

This emotional or "instinctive" telepathy may occur between unthinking and undeveloped beings, between humans and animals and in some cases between animals, in addition to the interplay between average humans. It is not a transmission of thoughts and words but of feelings. Menace, fear, friendliness, harmlessness or love may all be experienced in this way. Such communication exists between mother and child and is the manner in which the emotional body of the child is created by its parents just as surely as is the physical body. It is found in the theatre, when the star sways the audience and makes them laugn or cry. In this case the individuals in the audience also exchange emotional reactions with each other in response to the stimulus provided by the performer, and it is one of the reasons why they are likely to panic if fire or any other danger threatens. It is also this type of telepathy which is found dominating the average spiritualistic seance. The people are urged to sit close together sometimes with hands or arms touching to form a circle. This facilitates the free flow of solar plexus energy throughout the group. Their feelings, worries, sorrows and desires become apparent and are introduced as part of the so-called reading.

This emotional telepathy was the earliest mode of communication between man and man and antedated speech. Originally it concerned itself only with self-preservation and self-production and manifested chiefly as a type of inner sensation. Today it still lingers in a higher form and you have often heard "I have a feeling this is going to happen" or "I felt you were going to call."

You should make a positive effort to elevate this type of sensitivity to a higher stage of feeling. Work toward communication from "heart to heart" and thus develop a compassionate interest in others.

Mental Telepathy

The second type of telepathic communication between individuals, that from the mind of one to the mind of another, is what we are concerned with here. Let me point out to you at the very outset that the more thoroughly emotion and feeling and strong desire are eliminated, the more accurate and successful will your experiment become. Actually, the strong desire to achieve success in telepathic work or the fear of failure is a sure way to neutralize the very best effort. Any emotion in the receiver tends to create streams of energy which radiate out from him and act as a shield or buffer which prevent the incoming mental energies from making contact. In somewhat the same manner worry or anxiety on the part of the sender will turn his outgoing thought back on himself like a boomerang.

Therefore the first consideration should be the attainment of the proper attitude. Try to cultivate a spirit of "don't care" or non-attachment. Emotionally you should feel that it is not important to you whether the experiment succeeds or not. This is another way of saying that your attention or your consciousness should be focused in the mind and brain. This can best be achieved by a person who has learned to concentrate and direct his thoughts, as described in the chapter on thought. I must assume you have undertaken these preliminary steps and are prepared to proceed.

Today, the capacity for mental telepathy is becoming increasingly evident. Instinctive telepathic work is still the easiest path for most and this possibility must always be watched for and guarded against. Not that it is wrong or bad, but it makes for confusion. The solar plexus is still exceedingly active in most of us and therefore the earliest successful attempts will usually be a mixture of emotional and mental telepathy. Frequently the sender will project a message quite properly through the throat center but the recipient with an active solar plexus will get it two ways. This results in an emotional interpretation of the message not intended, and not in the sender's mind, but solely in the aura of the recipient. For example, the sender may project the message "hurry," or "make haste," having in mind nothing more than the speeding up of the recipient's efforts to learn the telepathic process. The receiver, however, even though he correctly apprehends the idea of "make haste," is likely to surround it with all sorts of dire emotional pictures drawn from his own "worry" storehouse. He will experience a sense of frustration because he is not proceeding faster, he will fear he is failing because he is not fast enough, he will feel resentment at the circumstances which he believes retard his progress; in short he will find himself in a complete emotional turmoil because of the implied urgency in the message "make haste."

Thus you see how important it is to have developed your powers of concentration to a point where it is possible to hold the attention or consciousness on a mental level and dissolve or drop off all emotional interference. To have fruitful results the head centers of both sender and receiver must be consciously and deliberately employed. Likewise, both parties must be relaxed and ready. If one party is under an emotional strain, he is very likely not to be properly responsive, although he may have the best intentions. Or again, if one or the other is occupied with a mental problem of his own he may be encased in a wall of thought forms which will effectively prevent any message from either getting out or coming in.

There are many problems, as you can well realize, and the cultivation of a form of detachment is essential to success. However, let us assume that we are successful in this and proceed to the next step.

It has been said that a good telepathic interrelation will grow through the medium of a constant attitude of reflective thought and a steadfast love for each other. Now "love" here does not refer to personal physical love but to its higher counterpart, which recognizes all personality weaknesses and failings but dismisses them as unimportant in relation to the shining light of the true inner self. These two factors of reflective thought and steadfast love cannot be developed overnight and they are not possible between any two given persons. They represent an ultimate, an ideal, and we are only at the beginning. But we must make a start, so what is needed is a technique.

In planning this technique we must bear in mind that in telepathy we are dealing with matter and energy in just the same way as when we build a house or construct a railroad. True, we deal with a different type of energy and a much finer grade of matter, but they are still matter and energy and obey the laws of matter and energy. Always remember this.

The Technique of Telepathy

In telepathy we will be dealing with (1) the force of love, (2) the force of mind and (3) primal energy, in the following manner:

1. The force of love attracts the needed material with which to clothe the idea, thought or concept to be transmitted, thus producing a coherency. You must realize that when you conceive an idea or frame a mental concept you are actually

gathering together and compressing into one place a portion of primal energy. In order to hold that portion together long enough for it to be transmitted to another, you must encase it in a capsule or compress it together in some way. This is where the force of love is needed, for love is a magnetic or attractive force of great power and it causes the elements in the idea to cohere for a length of time that is in direct ratio to the amount of love force supplied.

The force of love is also used by the recipient to attract the thought form or idea or message to himself after it has been released by the sender. This is done by the recipient's concentrating on the sender in a loving way and sending the warmth of his love to the sender. You can see from this how difficult a transmission would become if the slightest dislike or disapproval was permitted to exist between the sender and recipient. This is why such emphasis is placed upon loving and non-critical attitude.

2. The force of mind is necessary to literally "light the way" for an idea or thought form to be transmitted and received. While this simile of light is nearer to the actual manifestation, it will probably be clearer if I liken the mind to the telephone company which, after receiving the number from the sender, proceeds to select the proper lines and connections out of the many million available—the exact lines which will make the connection with the recipient. In fact, light is used. It is a most subtle substance as well as a very obvious one, and the energy of the mind can materialize on a beam of light. In the last year or so scientists have been experimenting with the idea of modulating laser beams in much the same manner that a radio wave is modulated and sent out by a broadcasting station. Herein is a most important clue to successful mental telepathic communication. A so-called line-of-sight alignment or a tube of light (like a laser beam) is set up between the brains and minds of the sender and recipient. The light from the sender's mind must project like a beam or beacon and upon this ray the message will travel truly to its intended mark. Of course, the re-

cipient must exert the magnetic power of love to attract attention, produce an alignment and create attunement.

3. The primal energy inherent in the vital body of the receiver reacts to the energies of love and will as they make their dual impact. This causes the recipient's brain to first become passive and receptive and then gradually awaken to a response activity. The message or idea is then swept into the area of conscious awareness and realized by the recipient. I might point out here that as you advance in this work you will frequently experience a "delayed action." If you are close to some person, or have been working telepathically with a person, he may send you a message at a time not previously arranged. You may be involved in work or in some other way at the time and your attention completely focused on what you are doing. In such cases the message may be properly received and stored and then released at a later time in your conscious mind when it is at rest.

Having in mind the foregoing, the technique to be employed should be as follows. The sender must:

1. Send out love to the recipient while visualizing his face or name.
2. Focus his full attention on the mental level and quiet all emotions.
3. Visualize the message or idea.
4. Then send it forth on a stream of love to the recipient.
5. Dismiss all thought of the process from his mind with the feeling that the communication has been successfully transmitted.

The recipient should:

1. Send out a stream of love to the sender. This can be visualized as if he were reaching out his hand to touch him, and at the same time feeling the warmth of love for him.
2. By use of the will, lift his consciousness to the mental level and hold it there, free from all emotional stress.
3. Relax and assume an attitude of indifference, not eagerness.

This releases the psychic energy in his body, to be impressed and molded by the incoming thought form.

There you have it. That is the technique, the whole technique. It seems simple—it is simple. The only difficult part is in training the mind, the emotions and the body to play the right part at the right time. This is like learning to paint or play the piano. Control is involved and this takes practice and work.

In the beginning it will be best if the sender and recipient are in the same room or in adjoining rooms. Then the sender can notify the receiver when he is starting to send by giving a signal such as a tap of a pencil or the sounding of a bell, and can give some corresponding signal when he finishes. To start, a simple visualization is best. Let the sender picture in his mind a clear-cut geometric figure, such as a circle, a triangle, a square or a star. Tell the recipient in advance it will be a geometric figure in order to facilitate the opening of the channel. Obviously this type of advance warning has no place in true telepathic transmission, but in the beginning it is important to facilitate matters in order to establish confidence.

The sender should be able to get a good clear visualization in about thirty seconds. He should try to hold it for about another thirty seconds, not more, then release it and put it out of his mind. Sometimes it helps to draw these symbols on pieces of paper, one symbol to one sheet, and then hold that one sheet only before the eye of the sender to help him see it clearly in his mind's eye. In fact, it is a good idea for the sender not to see any of the other symbols for at least five minutes before he starts to send. The mind is an odd instrument when it is not completely understood, and it is quite possible for the sender to be looking at one symbol and be thinking of another if he is not careful.

As pointed out earlier, do not try hard to do this. A relaxed and "I-don't-care" attitude is best. Never work at it for more than thirty minutes at first, and only extend that time when you are achieving obvious success. Then you can start sending more complex messages. At first try actual pictures. Have the sender look at a picture in a magazine, an advertisement for example, and after it has been projected ask the receiver to (a) describe the picture, or (b) tell what colors were in it, or (c) what objects could be discerned. As you realize, this is quite a sophisticated transmission and requires both skill and a good degree of attunement. Try words and sentences also and proceed to make this more complicated as you find that the simple words are easily registered.

After you have achieved a degree of success working with a companion in the same room, try sending and receiving at a distance. Select a person in another part of the city, or better still in another city, and decide on a specific day and time for the experiment. Do not spend more than ten minutes sending or trying to receive. Then stop and check for results. This can be done by telephone or mail. Keep working with this until you succeed. It is no more difficult than working with someone in the same room, but you may find it so because of your imagination. In the medium you are using distance is not a factor, but in the physical it is. Since all of your conscious acts are limited by time and distance, it is easy to fall into the trap of believing that your mental transmission and reception will be so impeded. Once you overcome this idea, you will find it just as quick and easy as transmission in the same room.

A Demonstration of Telepathy—Picture Transmission

The Rosicrucian Lodges in various cities have classes in telepathy about once a month. The students usually are beginners who are being trained in the proper technique of reception. An advanced member skilled in sending images, will preside over the class and conduct the instruction. He does not attempt a one-to-one relationship as described earlier but radiates the image in all directions, not unlike the broadcasting from a television station. A great variety of exercises are given which make it possible to emphasize different aspects of reception. Let me describe one of these sessions.

The sender, in this case a woman, a practicing psychologist, presided over the class and acted as sender. She stood on a platform which was raised about a foot above floor level and the students, about sixty of them, sat in chairs facing her. Before her was a lectern and on it, seen only by herself, was a picture in full color, an advertisement which she had clipped from a current magazine. Mountains, sharp cascades of rock, dominated the picture, with green trees part-way up their slopes and a blue lake at their feet. When all the students were comfortably seated, the teacher opened the class.

She began with a short lecture on the principle and laws involved, explaining that she would gaze intently at a picture and register each detail of that picture in her mind. Then she would energize with love the reflection of the picture in her consciousness and by the power of her will radiate it outward. She said, "I will concentrate on this picture for three minutes until I am sure I have included all its details in the image I am about to create; then for the next three minutes I will send the picture to you, to all of you. In order to put you in a receptive mood and raise your vibrations from the nagging physical and emotional turbulence which you have brought along with you from your busy day, we will first intone the vowel sound AUM three times on the note of D natural above middle C. Now sit comfortably and relax and when the intonation is completed I will proceed immediately to the experiment."

The note of D was struck on the piano and all present sang out the AUM in full voice. To a person not acquainted with the procedure it probably sounded like a mixed group of poorly trained voices at choir practice. But the effect was different. As the last, lingering sound of the third intonation died away, a quiet and peace settled over the group and a slight charging of the atmosphere in the room became noticeable. In this electric silence the experiment started.

For six minutes all was still. No one coughed, no one moved. Each student was relaxed but intensely aware. Finally the sender looked up, smiled and said,

"Who got anything?"

Immediately hands went up all over the room. The newest and

least experienced were the first, as usual. One said, "I saw mountains," and when the instructress smiled and nodded assent he was encouraged and added, "Blue mountains."

"No, they are not blue," he was told, "but there is blue in the picture."

"I know," said another, "there is blue sky beyond the mountains and the water in the foreground reflects the blue as well."

"Good!" said the teacher, "That is a very clear pick up. Now, someone else?"

And so it went all over the room, some adding details correctly, some mentioning items that were not in the picture at all. An example of how errors creep in came when one young man said, "I saw a frosted glass full of reddish brown liquid with the name Coca-Cola across it." The teacher said "No. That is not in the picture," but almost simultaneously a young man nearby, another student, said, "Oh, I guess that is my fault. My mind was wandering and being thirsty, I thought how good a long, cool drink would be. I guess I must have accompanied the wish with a picture of what I had in mind."

"Obviously you did," said the instructress dryly. "Anyone else?"

Before long, not more than fifteen minutes, the entire picture was described in all its details. As far as could be observed, no one student saw the picture in entirety, but the group together certainly did. The colors, the green of the trees, the slate gray of the rocks, the two peaks jutting skyward, the blue of the sky above and the lake below, were seen by many, the tiny configurations and minute details by but a few. This was a typical training session, not an unusual or difficult performance but one designed to instruct the new students and most of all to give them the confidence that they, too, can actually receive mental impressions from another.

There is no doubt that at first this can be done more easily and more successfully in such a group of like-minded students working under the direction of a skilled instructress, but it may also be done by you, working with one other person or with a small group. Do not attempt more than three or four at first. Everyone has his own ideas and his own emotional problems and where there are too many untrained minds present, no satisfactory results can be expected.

Verbal Telepathic Communication

The foregoing experiment involved the transmission of a picture. No ideas or messages were included. Sending a picture is simpler and easier than trying to transmit a message or an idea. A picture is a direct visual experience. There is no mistaking what you see and this makes possible a certain "purity" of sending which is much more difficult to attain when you try to transmit a message. A message involves words and words in themselves are symbols. A double process is therefore required at each end, the idea or thought must be couched in words which accurately express it in the mind of the sender; the word or words are then sent and when received they must be decoded by the receiver and translated back into ideas or thoughts. Even when this has been done, there is no guarantee that your interpretation of the word received is the one with which the sender intended to endow it when it was sent to you.

It is true, this hazard also exists in oral speech, but to a lesser degree. A single word is seldom spoken. Usually there is a rush of language, with each word supported by the ones that preceded it and those that follow, and all are enhanced by intonation and the magic of the speaker's personality.

Because of this more involved technique in verbal telepathy and the increased possibility of error, the training is much more rigorous. You must begin with single words. Not before you have acquired assurance in sending one word at a time can you contemplate sending sentences, much less complete ideas. Patanjali, the great Hindu Sage and Teacher, recommends the following technique:

1. Study the form of the word; study it symbolically as a word picture.
2. Study it from the angle of quality, of beauty, of desire.
3. Study its underlying purpose and teaching value as well as its mental appeal.

4. Study its very being and attempt to identify yourself with its divine underlying idea.

As you can see, the process gradually lifts your consideration of the word to ever-higher levels in your consciousness. When you have achieved the highest possible, then send out the word to the receiver, who in turn should endeavor to maintain his attention on the highest mental level of which he is capable. In sending, it is frequently helpful if the sender will actually articulate the word softly and clearly as he releases it from his consciousness.

The art of communicating with one another has come a long way. It started with the sense of touch a million, maybe two million years ago. The next step was sound, not words but cries of joy, of pain, gurgles of ecstasy, groans of anguish. Next came symbols, gestures of the arms and body, indications of the head. The sign language of the American Indian is a sophisticated out-growth of this earlier method of communication by signs, which antedated speech. Hundreds of thousands of years elapsed be-tween the first groping efforts to communicate by touch and the articulation of words. Words then grew into sentences and sentences into language. Eventually writing developed, first as a representation of the gestures of sign communication, then as pictures of events. Finally these earlier pictures became con-ventionalized into letters and words.

The various arts marked man's next step upward in his efforts to convey his thoughts and impressions to others. Sculpture, crude at first, then becoming more stylized, followed by music and then by painting and poetry. This is where the world stands today. The higher means of communication still to be mastered are telepathy, which we study here, inspiration and eventually illumination. Yes, these last are forms of communication, as you will realize if you consider them for a moment. True, they are not the man-to-man communication of telepathy, but refer to a man's ability to make contact with and draw upon realms of knowledge beyond our most fantastic imagining. Illumination comes only as a result of tremendous control and vast develop-ment. This is well beyond the average individual. But everyone above a certain mental level does experience flashes of inspiration. This latent ability can be developed, and I will give you some suggestions in Chapter Twelve on how you may do this.

To recapitulate, let me say that successful mental telepathy depends upon the following:

1. The channel between the sender and receiver must be kept open. Any criticism spoken or only implied, any suspicion or resentment of one for the other, any impatience or irritation on the part of either, will break the contact.

2. The sender must concentrate on sending. There will be many temptations to let his mind wander, even to think overmuch of the receiver or the technique being employed. The receiver should be designated in an early visualization, then put out of the mind while the entire effort is to visualize with clarity and then release with love the message to be sent.

3. For his part, the receiver should think of the sender for just a moment or two and then after sending him a wave of love-attraction, put the personality out of mind. From that point onward the receiver must be truly detached if maximum success is to be achieved. He must maintain what can best be described as a "don't-care" attitude. Any anxiety about failure or a strong desire for success will be self-defeating.

4. Possibly the greatest difficulty the receiver will encounter is the quieting of his own thoughts. As long as they are active the energy they generate will radiate and create a magnetic wall which will block out any incoming thought energy. The receiver must learn how to relax his mind, must indeed practice this beforehand and become proficient in order to insure success.

You are ready to learn telepathy. You have probably had many experiences with telepathic contact, some of which you recognized, some not. This is a faculty inherent in all humans and requires only attention and practice for its development. The human race needs to relearn telepathy and within 500 years it will again become an accepted mode of communication for a large, a very large, segment of humanity. You are ready for it

now and can learn it through conscientious effort and hard practice. If you set yourself to do this and are successful you will
benefit yourself in many ways, but what is even more important,
you will be contributing to the advancement of the entire human
race. I urge you to be a pioneer. The rewards are very great.

ELEVEN

How to Generate and Apply Psychic Energy

Earlier in the book is was pointed out that we live in a sea of energy almost like fish live in water, except that this energy interpenetrates us completely. Now we will examine this energy and in particular one specific type which the Rosicrucians refer to as soul or psychic energy.

We are dual beings. Our physical body is animated by physical energy and we are led normally to thoughts, desires and actions which add to the well-being of this body. But we are also led quite frequently to perform actions which appear to be contrary to our body's best interests. A hungry mother gives her last morsel of food to her child, a man risks and sometimes loses his life to save another, a soldier bravely faces almost certain death to capture an enemy stronghold. It would be difficult to prove that any one of these acts is good for the body. Yet similar deeds are performed daily by people all over the world, usually with the approval and often the applause of their fellowmen. Why is this?

The answer you know. We do not regard ourselves as mere physical entities. We understand that our physical equipment is inhabited and guided by a more subtle form of energy which we call the soul and this soul has different objectives and different ideals from the body. Frequently these appear at cross-purposes and cause inner conflict. Sometimes this is decided in favor of the physical, at other times the soul's preferences prevail. All the foregoing is obvious and I mention it only to emphasize what is too often overlooked.

The soul clearly has objectives of its own, some of which seem to be decidedly contrary to our (physical) best interests. It has also the power to drive people to achieve these objectives and, what is more, to make those objectives seem so desirable and praiseworthy that others applaud the one who strives to obtain them. Have you ever stopped to consider how much energy this takes? An energy which drives people, millions of people, to act against their own welfare, health and security must be powerful indeed. As you consider this are you not impressed with the great power of the soul? But do you use it? Have you ever tried to use it? Very few people consciously use or even try to use psychic energy. Yet most of us respond to and are used by it. The Rosicrucians teach the nature of this remarkable energy, the laws under which it functions and how we may employ it. When it said in the Bible that man was given dominion over all creation it meant just that. We have the power. It is up to us to learn how to use it.

To the beginner his attempts to employ psychic energy are like trying to hold a handful of water; the harder he grasps, the less he retains. At the start therefore it is better to direct this energy to someone else. You will have quicker success and it is safer too. Until you understand and know how to use it, the more psychic energy you draw to yourself, the more problems you will have. All energy is from the same Source and is therefore basically the same. At the Source it is exceedingly fine and vibrates at an unbelievably high rate. As it makes its way down to the physical level it becomes progressively less tenuous and its vibratory rate lowers. The psychic energy which you may accumulate has this same descending tendency and, like rain falling upon a field, it fills all the holes and lower spots first. It need not, but to delay this downward progress you must know how to capture and hold it. If you do not, all facets of your nature will be stimulated and the most powerful (the largest holes in the field), your greatest weaknesses in other words, will get the most energy and receive the greatest stimulation. This is the reason why so many would-be mystics and students of the occult seem to become evil instead of good. They begin to attract psychic energy but only a small portion of what they obtain is used to stimulate their minds and higher emotions. The bulk of it drifts on down into the lower emotions and physical appetites and in a short time these people whose original intentions were of the best become egotistical, dogmatic, power hungry and in some cases even lecherous and dissolute. Energy is energy. It's what is done with it that makes the difference.

The soul understands the energy of its own level and uses it to raise the consciousness of men. We are not meant to live as animals. Gradually the energy poured into us by our souls is lifting up humanity. But we still have a long way to go and anything you can do to speed up this process within yourself or for others is helpful and praiseworthy. Compare the average level of awareness and understanding today with that of one thousand years ago and consider the change that has taken place. True, we still lean heavily on violence to achieve national objectives but even here the weight of popular thinking is beginning to tell. Most other accepted cruelties and barbarisms have been eliminated or greatly inhibited. No longer is "an eye for an eye" and "a tooth for a tooth" the highest known form of justice, but mercy and understanding are beginning to show themselves in man's dealings with his fellow creatures. If such great changes have already occurred can we complacently assume there are no more to come? Should we not be encouraged to believe the surface of man's abilities has barely been scratched and that the days to come will produce far more remarkable changes and improvements?

The Rosicrucians say so and offer as proof the lessons and techniques which enable an earnest student to unfold remarkable hidden abilities in his own nature. One of these is a method for acquiring, retaining and employing psychic energy. I should not emphasize the way we get psychic energy because this is a normal process. We acquire it all the time in the air we breathe. True, this can be speeded up and I will explain how. But a real technique is required to retain and control this energy after you have obtained it. Normally, we misuse and dissipate it as fast as we get it. These pitfalls must be avoided and when you learn where they lie, you can avoid them.

Speeding up the Accumulation of Psychic Energy

There are many ways in which you can speed up the accumulation of psychic energy. There are some substances that store it. Pine needles, particularly the short, new green shoots, will radiate this energy into your finger tips. Just touch the tip of each finger and thumb to the points of the needles and hold them in that position for two or three minutes. This will give you a slight charge of psychic energy and if repeated daily, two or three times each day for a few weeks, there will be a noticeable strengthening in your aura and your entire etheric-mental nature. This is a particularly good treatment for people who have been sick or are run down and their energies are at low ebb. The treatment should be practiced with the bough still growing on the tree and not cut off from it.

Another very helpful ingredient is musk. U.S.P. musk can be purchased from most high-grade drug suppliers. The best musk came originally from China and there is still some on the market. I believe a Tibetan musk is now being imported. All musk is expensive, usually about $100 an ounce. But no great amount is needed. A half ounce kept well sealed in a bottle will last a long time since only two or three grains are taken at one time. The musk should be in tiny, dark granules and have a slightly aromatic odor. It should also be very slightly oily in appearance. A dosage consists of two or three grains, which may be taken by moistening the tip of a finger and then dipping it into the container. A few granules will adhere to the moist fingertip, and these are sufficient. Since musk has a most pronounced stimulating effect, no more than two doses should be taken in any one day and never within three hours of retiring. The ancient kings and rulers in India and China took musk before making any serious decision involving the welfare of their country, believing that its potency sharpened their brains and enabled them to think more clearly. You can do the same.

Let me remind you again at this point that the energy you may thus acquire will go where you send it or where it is led. Do not make the mistake of increasing your psychic energy and then permit it to be wasted in physical indulgence. This road leads to disaster.

The easiest, simplest and most usual method of increasing psychic energy is by means of the breath. Yes, your breath, but not by ordinary, normal breathing. The energy is acquired by retaining the breath in the lungs for a specified period and then when it is released by allowing it to vibrate or rasp over the root of the palate as you let it out through your nose with your mouth closed. The explanation is that the air, our atmosphere, is charged with many grades and levels of energy. When you breathe normally and rhythmically without conscious attention, the energy you acquire is the positive counterpart of the so-called negative energy you have taken into your system in the form of food and drink. Without the energy of the air to complete it, this negative energy is useless in the human machine—no air, no energy, and the machine soon ceases to function. The same is true if the positive energy of air is supplied but the negative energy from food and drink is not. The end may not be so quick because the human system stores a great deal of food and water in its tissues and as long as this holds out you live—but when it is exhausted you die.

Normally, this physical energy is the only form you retain from the air you breathe, the energy which keeps you alive and able to feel, think and act. But there are many higher grades of energy in the air, some of which we can extract with but little practice. Others of higher quality require that our equipment first be refined and this takes time and effort. Let me first give you two techniques for extracting certain grades of psychic energy from the air and then let us discuss them. After that we can then speak of the higher grades and suggest methods of approach to them. Here is the first breathing technique:

1. Stand before an open window or out of doors or any place where you can get clear, fresh air.
2. Separate your feet and stretch your arms out horizontally at your sides.
3. Breathe in to the count of five.
4. Then immediately breathe out to the count of ten. Be sure

the counting is at the same pace for both in-breathing and out-breathing.

5. Repeat this breathing cycle ten times.

6. This exercise may also be performed with almost equal benefit while sitting erect in a chair or even while walking in the open.

For maximum benefit do this exercise at least once every day but two or three times will be better. It can be performed almost anywhere, in your home, at an office or while walking in the street.

It is well to begin with the foregoing breathing exercise but after a month you may add the following more sophisticated technique.

1. Sit comfortably in a chair. Hold your back straight and your head erect. Cross your feet at the ankles, not the knees, and hold them touching. Clasp your hands in your lap, or if you prefer, before your breast as if in prayer.

2. Take a deep breath through your nose and count rhythmically to yourself as you do. The intake should cover the period of eight counts. Pace it so, exactly.

3. Now hold your breath in your lungs for exactly twelve counts. Don't speed up and don't slow down. Count rhythmically.

4. Let the air out through your nose. Pace it to cover ten counts. With a little practice this is easy and after a while the timing will become so natural you won't have to count. As you breathe out consciously direct the flow of outgoing air to the spot where it enters the nasal passage from the throat. This is about at the root of the palate. Feel the air going past this sensitive spot and accompany the flow of air with a slightly audible vibration like a purring or humming sound. Continue this consciously induced vibration as long as the air continues its outward flow.

5. Repeat the foregoing five times.

If you take into your lungs more air than is needed to balance off the negative elements in the blood in the lungs and retain it longer than the balancing process requires, two things happen. First, the positive elements tend to dominate and turn the balance of your physical body to the positive side. Second, the finer energies in the air itself seek to manifest and since each human being has a built-in response mechanism for these energies, this mechanism starts to function. You then begin to accumulate psychic energy, and you will acquire some each time you do this. At first only a little, but as you continue to practice your interior equipment will limber up and become more efficient. The slight vibration at the base of your palate during the exhaling speeds this up.

This exercise should be performed in its entirety at least once a day and it may be used three or four times a day. After you have gone through it once, test it. Separate your hands and then bring them close without touching. Cup your palms and, with thumbs opposing, bring each finger close to its corresponding finger on the other hand. Keep them about a half inch apart and breathe normally. You will then feel the energy, which will tingle at your finger tips. If the room is dark and you have a mirror before you, you will see a bluish haze between your hands. This is psychic energy. Now that you have accumulated some extra energy of high quality, learn how to conserve it and use it properly. Do not debase it and don't throw it away.

I cannot dwell enough on the ways we all waste energy. If a complete tabulation were attempted it could fill several books. In general though, the greatest waste for the average person comes from indulging the lower emotions, appetites and passions. If you like power, if this is your weakness, the additional psychic energy will enable you to gain a little more power and once this is gained you will want more and more. This will cause you to become dissatisfied and unhappy unless you awaken to your error and correct it. The same or a similar road lies before the vain and proud and an equally difficult path faces those who dissipate their psychic power in gratifying lower animal vices. Some people who believe they are circumspect and well controlled will pry into the lives of others. With only curiosity moving them and no loving desire to help, they will eavesdrop

and peer and speculate and question. What a waste of energy
this is!

How to Prevent Loss of Psychic Energy

Some people draw energy from you, just as others stimulate
you and appear to give you energy. There is an exchange of
energy going on all the time between humans. The artist on the
stage draws energy from the audience, a small amount from each
person but in the aggregate very stimulating to him. An acknowl-
edged leader like the commanding officer of a regiment or the
manager of a business receives energy from those who are subject
to his direction, a small amount, true, but the aggregate will
equal the sum of his authority. People who love each other are
constantly giving energy to each other and this strengthens both.
There are many ways in which energy is given and taken and
sometimes just thrown away. The important point for you is to
protect yourself from unnecessary losses.

The solution lies in what is described as "containment." You
must consciously gather your forces together, like gathering a
cloak around you, and hold them there, resisting the temptations
and impulses to send them hither and yon on all sorts of wild
goose chases. Do not permit your eyes to be caught by and to
follow each passing movement. Do not let your mind be captured
and led astray by every vagrant thought. Contain yourself and
your precious energies.

"Containment" is achieved by conscious effort. You must not
only restrain yourself from squandering energy; you must prevent
it from slipping away. If you are lazy and slothful your psychic
energy will gradually leave you and only its physical counterpart
will remain. A certain tension must be maintained, and this is
best accomplished by energetic activity throughout your waking
hours. Not continuous physical activity, of course, although this
is good and will accomplish the desired objective. Better is the
effort of mental concentration, which creates greater tension and
more efficient containment.

The Fiery World of Psychic Energy

We call this world of higher energies the fiery world. This is because the element of fire most nearly represents to our consciousness the action of psychic energy. Our scientists have come a long way in a very short time. They now know that different types of atoms contain different energies and that these energies can be released. Some of these new atomic energies are entirely different from any heretofore measured and used by science. When they are classified and their properties put to work a great change will come about in human living. Right now we are completely enthralled by physical concepts. Our best efforts to employ atomic energy ignore the unique potentials which the various elements store in their atomic structure and are aimed solely at converting their great power into simple heat energy. The Masters of Wisdom smile at this misapplication even while they deplore the fact that the best values are being thrown away. But it will not be too many years before certain more imaginative researchers will begin to discover and understand the hidden properties and when they are finally put to use, destitution will be ended and every human alive will have a comfortable living assured.

Up to the present it has been human energy that has kept the human race alive. In recent years, since about the middle of the Nineteenth Century, the energies of the sun in the soil and in minerals have made a substantial contribution, but these have fallen under the control of aggressive and selfish men, which has resulted in riches for a few and poverty for many. Today this is being balanced out to some degree through political devices but tomorrow, when the fiery energies of the atoms are employed, there will be so much more energy available that human toil will no longer be necessary. There will be so much that all, even the most greedy, will have plenty. This "utopia" will not come about quickly and easily. All change is ever opposed by reactionary forces and the powers entrenched against these developments are the greatest in the world. So we will have to wait.

While the basic elements—earth, water and air—are obviously present in all things, mineral, vegetable, animal and human, the element of fire is considered by most people to be different and present only under special circumstances. Yet fire interpenetrates and pervades all things and is more vitally present than any of the other three. It is everywhere in various guises and in different degrees. It is the cohesive force and energizing power. All creative action is fiery action. Fire heals and destroys. Fire is present on the physical, etheric, emotional and mental planes, and of course on the plane of the soul, too, where it is manifested as the power of love.

We know of the subtle world. It is not too difficult to make contact with and consciously enter it. The fiery world, the world of psychic energy, exists in the same manner as the subtle world but its state is much finer. It is as far beyond the subtle world as the subtle is beyond and different from the physical. The physical world exists right here on earth and on other material spheres similar to this planet. The subtle world exists in the envelope which surrounds our world and similar heavenly bodies but the fiery world interpenetrates all worlds and all the space between them. It is not only vaster than our visible universe but fuller and far more complete. There are no barren wastes, no empty spots, no vacuums. All of the intervening space (if you can call it that) between here and anywhere you can imagine is literally teeming with living energy more complex and richer than anything we know.

Don't make the mistake of thinking that fire as we know it, or electricity, or lightning is a direct manifestation of psychic energy. It is not. It is but a crystallization (so to speak) of physical energy. We can see fire and lightning and feel them burn and hear the sounds they produce, and therefore they are physical and belong in the realm of our five senses. Psychic energy is more subtle and vibrates at a higher rate.

There are two avenues of approach to the fiery world—the personal, which is taught by the Rosicrucians and described in brief here, and the scientific, impersonal approach, which it remains for the future to disclose. Actually many apparatuses are possible of creation right today, apparatuses which would enable many to open the door to the fiery world, but the consciousness of mankind, steeped in ignorance and superstition will not permit it.

Some Examples of Psychic Energy

Until you have had the experience of consciously contacting and employing psychic energy, most descriptions sound vague and unsatisfying. So let me give you some examples which will enable you to relate this energy to your own experience.

Most of the strange and mystifying occurrences that seem to be contrary to all physical law as we know it are the result of action of psychic energy in one form or another. There are literally hundreds of types and a complete compendium is well beyond the scope of this work. But we can examine two or three of the more common manifestations and the understanding you gain will enable you to comprehend most others.

Dowsing. The New York Times of October 13, 1967, carries the following headline in bold type on page 17.

DOWSERS DETECT ENEMY'S TUNNELS

The article, written by Hanson W. Baldwin, was datelined Camp Pendleton, California, and described how Marine Corps engineers both in their training program in California and under actual battle conditions in Vietnam were using improvised divining rods to detect tunnels, mines and booby traps. Usually ordinary wire coat hangers are used. They are first straightened out and then bent into an L, with one end about twenty-six inches and the other about eight inches in length. The operator takes a wire in each hand, holding the short ends lightly in his fists with the longer ends standing out in front of him, parallel to each other.

The reporter, Baldwin, observed several experiments and even made a successful trial run himself. When the ends tend to separate and spring apart, it indicates there is a tunnel directly beneath; over a buried mine the ends point down, etc. Major

Nelson Hardacker of the Fifth Marine Division stated that the device would not work for some men but they were in the minority. Baldwin said he tried it and located a tunnel whose existence he had not suspected. In his case one rod sloped down and Major Hardacker explained that this indicated the tunnel had a downward slope at that point.

This is not a new discovery but a very ancient practice called "dowsing" and in some areas "water-witching," because in the vast majority of instances it has been used to find water. In its primitive form this practice employed a forked twig or branch. It is centuries old and records of it have been found among Roman writings. Originally it was considered magical by the superstitious, and its adepts were feared by some and held in awe by others. Usually knowledge of the art was kept in certain families and handed down from father to son but today we know that most people can achieve fair results with a little practice.

The traditional method of dowsing was for the practitioner to cut a small forked branch from a tree and trim it down until it formed a Y about two feet from tip to tip. He would then grasp the two arms of the Y and hold the branch out in front of him with the main stem extending forward parallel to the ground. In this manner he would traverse the area back and forth where it was hoped a well might be dug. When the tip of the stem vibrated and bobbed down toward the ground, a mark was made and the process repeated from another direction. In this way the repetition and vigor of the stick's movements would determine an optimum spot, which was usually found to be correct.

This technique has been practiced all over the world for more than two thousand years and today it is more in use than ever before. Not only water but oil and minerals are sought in the ground in this way. The primitive hazel twig has given way to divining rods of metal and plastic. The professional dowser (and there are many) will usually carry with him two or three different types and at least one of them will be a compact folding instrument that he can keep in his breast pocket.

At first this practice was regarded as magical or at the very least done by departed spirits. Then, when it became apparent that everyday experimenters like you and me could also make the rod or twig "work," more rational explanations were sought. Most dowsers have no idea how they do it. It just works. However, each one has a theory and together these theories cover a lot of territory. It is impossible to list and describe them all but, as you can imagine, some are pretty fantastic. The most popular explanations hinge upon (1) the idea that the dowser has a special animal magnetism that is affected by the nearness of water or oil, and (2) that the water running through the ground creates a magnetic field which attracts the divining rod, and (3) a combination of the two.

Of course certain scientists—respected, successful geologists—maintain to this day that dowsing is nonsense and the results achieved come from previous knowledge of the location or lucky guesses. But they are in the minority and the vast number of successful "findings" far outweighs the prestige of the degrees of these die-hards. Of course running water does create a magnetic field, and the many scientists who accept dowsing lean heavily on this factor. However, just when everything seemed in order and the explanations were satisfactory to all concerned, a new element intruded itself. It seemed that when a dowser set out to find oil on a location, his divining rod indicated where oil was to be found, but if he was looking for water it would locate water for him. This disturbed the magnetic field theory and while it did not disprove it, it certainly indicated that there are other factors which must be considered.

It was about this time that certain successtul dowsers with more than the usual amount of curiosity started their experiments with maps. Using a pendulum instead of a divining rod, they were able to locate lost mines, wells and even ancient sewers on maps without going near the location in person.

A prime example is that of the island of Bermuda. From earliest times, this island was considered to have no underground water and depended entirely upon collected rainfall. This was adequate for its original small population but its popularity as a winter resort brought about a vast increase in visitors in the last few years, so more water was needed and lots of it.

Geologists were brought in and they confirmed the earlier opinions. However because of real estate developments and military needs several expensive dry holes were dug. Finally, one concern, hearing of dowsing, wrote to a well-known Maine dowser and offered him a good fee and his expenses if he would attempt to find water on the island. His reply surprised them. He said if they would just send him a large-scale map he would mark off five likely locations, which he did. Water was found at all five locations he marked, and the island now has plenty.

This additional element of mystery now has all the scientific minds completely confused. But, as you can see, the real energy here employed is becoming evident. It cannot be magnetism or any other physical energy, because it works at a distance and responds to thought. It must be and is psychic energy. The water and the oil and the ores in the ground all have their own magnetic aura. The psychic energy of the dowser, directed by his thought, reaches out toward the aura of the object sought, contacts it, locates it and represents its location to the dowser in the manner which he prescribes. This may be in the swinging of a pendulum or the bobbing of a stick. Successful dowsers all know they employ energy. They may not understand the type of energy they use but they are aware that when they feel strong and "light" they are more accurate than on days when they feel heavy and sluggish. When they finish an arduous session they usually feel depleted and want to rest. One famous dowser said to me that he worked best in places where the air was fresh and sweet and where he could take good deep breaths.

As to how to dowse, no practice or previous training are necessary. Just cut yourself a forked stick and start. True, you will need psychic energy, so take some deep breaths to get yourself positively charged first. You will learn by doing. Dowsing is but one of the many manifestations of the power of psychic energy. Psychometry is another.

Psychometry. The dictionary defines psychometry as "divination by means of things touched." Psychic energy has the faculty of clinging to physical objects. A porous, loosely constructed substance such as a straw hat or a cotton blouse will retain but a small amount, and that only for a short time. Solid substances, particularly precious metals, will attract and hold energy a great deal longer. The energy may be picked up from any radiatory source, and as a rule this means a person or persons. We are always radiating energy. In fact one of our problems is that we radiate too much, throw it away, you might say. If we carry a gold watch or wear a gold ring for any length of time it will accumulate quite a bit of this energy we disburse, all of it colored and qualified by our emotions and thoughts.

Thus if you are sensitive to the impact of psychic energy you can learn quite a lot about a person merely by holding in your hand some object, preferably of a precious metal, that he or she has worn or carried. No cooperation on the part of the person is required. If you hold a ring or a watch or a brooch or some other metal object that has been associated with a person for a reasonable length of time, say a year or so, not only will his character be clear to you but even key scenes from his past will appear to re-enact themselves in your mind. It is almost as if this inanimate object became a link between your mind and that of its former bearer.

At a social gathering one evening, the hostess asked a woman guest, a close friend who was known to be a very good psychometrizer, to demonstrate her ability. The hostess had in mind the entertainment of her guests but it soon became evident that this was an exhibition of unusual and amazingly accurate probing into the lives of the persons present. Not once did she err. One man gave her a gold coin and implied that he carried it as a pocket piece. Upon taking it in her hand she immediately said, "You have had this less than a day. What is more, it has passed through many hands recently and the last person to have it for any length of time died last year." The man was amazed and admitted he had obtained the gold piece from a jeweler that very day as a present for his niece and knew nothing of its previous history. Other revelations were equally impressive. When I asked her to describe how this knowledge comes to her, the psychometrist said:

> I take in my hand the object presented, close my eyes and relax. I don't try to see anything; I just make myself ready. As a rule, however, scenes will start to appear almost immediately. They come alive like a three-dimensional motion

picture in sound and color. I seem to be in the scene, at least it appears to be all around me, yet I am not a participant, only an observer. As long as the scene holds my interest, if it is significant and I want to understand what is taking place, it plays along to a conclusion. However, the moment I lose interest and my attention wavers, it shifts to another. Sometimes the owner of the object will ask a question and then the scene which appears will relate to that question— not necessarily an answer but always offering information or a new viewpoint.

Sometimes an object is offered which has not been carried by anyone present. I recall one incident when a strange brass or bronze device was handed to me. I didn't look at it carefully—in fact, I rarely do—so I was not aware of its appearance when I took it in my hand and waited for a connection to be made. To my surprise the scene which unfolded was in the Near East, or so I judged from the appearance or dress of the people, and it was not contemporary. In fact, it seemed quite ancient. The owner of the device I took to be an Arab or a Syrian and he was a public official of some sort. The object I held was his official seal which he stamped on reports and tallies which were presented to him. Many scenes from his life ran before me and it would have been interesting to study them, but there was not enough time available. So I opened my eyes and gave the seal back to the man who had placed it in my hand. When I told him what I had seen he was most interested and said it confirmed what he had been able to find out. An archaeologist had found it embedded in a hardened clump of clay at the entrance to a cave in the Holy Land. The device on it, he had been told, was an ancient Assyrian symbol for the goddess of material wealth and indeed, it looked strangely like our own dollar sign. The face of the seal was oval and smooth except in the center, where the insignia had been engraved. The design was a snake entwined upon a vertical staff.

This charming and interesting woman told me many other experiences which space will not permit me to relate here. She is a Rosicrucian like myself and for many years has taken a great interest in psychometry. Her natural bent in this direction has been fostered and improved by the exercises given in the Rosicrucian monographs, and through daily practice she has become a competent psychometrist. Many people have this gift but few work to develop it. Yet even a small increase in their psychic energy will be rewarded by a marked improvement in results.

Much of so-called fortune-telling, where it is legitimate and not fraud, is related to psychometry. The ancient request, "Cross my palm with silver," was not only to guarantee payment in advance but it was also to give the operator an opportunity to pick up what she could from contact with silver that had been carried on the person of the enquirer. Psychic energy acts in many ways and it is unwise to attempt to classify every manifestation under a specific heading. We have five physical senses, so it is quite natural for us to try to interpret every event in terms of one or another of these avenues of knowledge. Yet experience indicates that many of the remarkable occurrences of today may have come about in ways completely unknown to us. Consider this same fortune-telling, for instance. Sometimes it is very accurate. How is it done? Is it mind-reading? Is it psychometry? Is it true precognition? Is it keen psychological insight? Is it guesswork? Is it a little bit of all the foregoing mixed up together? Or is it something of which we do not yet have workable knowledge? As far as I can determine it is sometimes one or another of the foregoing, sometimes combinations of two or more and sometimes something entirely beyond my experience.

However you may wish to define it, this ability to look into the life record of an individual is a remarkable demonstration of the power of psychic energy. But there are many other evidences equally impressive. To treat them exhaustively would require several volumes. We can but indicate a few and give a short description of each.

Teleportation. This is the ability to move physical objects from one place to another without physical means, to make objects appear where they were not before and to make them disappear from where they were. Many people have experiences with teleportation but since they seem to be beyond the realm of the usual, they are ignored or discounted. When such an occurrence is forced upon his attention, the average man will say to himself,

"I must be mistaken. I have probably forgotten or overlooked something."

It has been observed that many quite ordinary people have the ability to teleport small objects. Much of the so-called poltergeist phenomena has been traced to teen-aged children, usually girls who gleefully teleport all sorts of things in and out of their homes while appearing to be the most innocent and unoffending by-standers. The ability to teleport is a skill like any other accomplishment and it must be learned. If a child has the ability, he or she must have acquired it in a previous life and retained the memory. This memory is seldom sharp and clear and the child usually discovers his skill by accident. At first its practice is exciting and sometimes amusing, but his limited imagination can find no purposeful use for it, so it is gradually forgotten.

Teleportation, like dowsing and psychometry, uses psychic energy. Each art requires that the energy be employed in a specific way for which training is necessary. A good dowser will probably have no knowledge of psychometry or teleportation and may even regard them with distrust. The more psychic energy you build into yourself and retain, the easier it will be for you to acquire one of these so-called wild talents. But each has to be learned.

Precognition. As the name indicates, this is the ability to know about things before they happen. It is a modern name for prophecy. A great many people experience it but no one except a very highly evolved individual has control over it. The impressions comes in flashes, usually when least expected. Sometimes a person with a well-developed psychic envelope, such as Jeanne Dixon, will be able to see, when asked, certain imminent events in the future of others. But seldom can she see her own as clearly, and when she does the relevations come in unpremeditated glimpses. While many quite average people have flashes of precognition, it appears that the more highly developed individuals, those whose psychic centers are more open, experience them more often. An adept of the third degree, that is to say, one who has experienced the third major initiation, can look into the akashic records of the past at will, but even he can only see those future events which have actually crystallized.

The human race is constantly changing its future. The dire catastrophes seen quite clearly by the prophets of a hundred years ago manifest today as minor earthquakes or volcanic eruptions. It is always the unforeseen blows that are the heaviest. The verbal description of a future event seems enough in itself to change it. Thus the ancient wise ones were always silent about their creations. So there are no really good prophets. This is not a question of ability, which may be the highest, but of changes in action due to the decisions of free will. In our present stage of development, precognition is like a will-o-the-wisp, sometimes clear and true, sometimes false. Each person's line of existence stretches into the future as it does to the past. You may look ahead along the line of a comrade's life and see catastrophe. There is no need for you to assume this event also awaits you. The prophet can look only in the direction his own lifeline points. It may not coincide with yours.

Levitation. This gravity-defying performance was apparently a lot more common in ancient times than it is today. Yet occasionally even now one runs into evidence of the ability to lift the body into the air without artificial aid. Not long ago I saw a stage performer who could change her weight. It was no trick. Curious, I went to the stage when people were called from the audience and found to my surprise that I could lift her easily with one hand as she sat in a basket-like contrivance with a handle at the top. Yet on the scale her size indicated the 140 pounds it recorded was correct. She could levitate to a small degree.

I asked her how she did it and she either did not know or else could not express what she did know. She said, "It's a knack. My mother could do it and I can. You can just make yourself feel light in here," and she put her palm over her diaphram.

I asked, "Have you ever been able to lift yourself off the ground into the air?" and she answered, "No. I tried several times and although I felt very light once or twice I was never successful in actually getting off the ground. However, when I was younger, about eight or nine, I had no fear of heights and would jump off walls and down flights of stairs. I never came down hard, never hurt myself, but always floated down gently like a thistledown."

The Rosicrucians explain that levitation is an art which can be acquired. Again psychic energy comes into play. To levitate skillfully and successfully the physical organism must be purified. A diet is prescribed and one must be rid of all excess weight. Along with the physical training, mental exercises are recommended and, of course, an increase in psychic energy is essential. Those who have succeeded explain that it is not too difficult to repeat once achieved, not too unlike learning to swim.

We have examined here five unusual abilities which may be developed through the proper employment of psychic energy. These five—dowsing, psychometry, teleportation, precognition and levitation—are all very obviously physical abilities which are inherent in all men. For if they were not, it would not be possible for so many individuals of so many different races and places and with such different backgrounds of experience and culture to perform them. But let me assure you that they are but the least of the possibilities inherent in the control of psychic energy. For example, little is said about personality dominance, and for obvious reasons. Yet this power might also be looked upon as a by-product of psychic development.

A perfect example of complete personality dominance is given in one of the news stories sent by Helena Blavatsky to the "Russian Messenger" (Russki Vyestnik, 1880) from India. She was with a party of a dozen Europeans, mostly French and English, who were touring India in luxury as the guests of a wealthy Rajput Prince whom she referred to as "the Takur." They came to a large lake in the center of which was an island with an ancient castle, and since it was late afternoon, they decided to pitch camp in this delightful spot.

One of the group, a well-known French artist whom Mme. Blavatsky refers to only as Mr. Y—, was intrigued by the beauty of the spot and set up his easel to paint what he saw. They had been discussing Mesmer and this artist had stated neither Mesmer nor anyone else could hypnotize (or mesmerize) him. As he proceeded with his painting, the Takur sat nearby smoking a pipe and watching. The discussion went on and Mr. Y— continued to paint while the servants set up tents and prepared the evening meal.

When dinner was announced one of the group, an Englishwoman referred to as Miss X—, said to the artist "I must see your painting" and walked over to look. Whereupon the rest of the group did likewise. "What an interesting painting!" said Miss X—. "Did you paint it from memory?" It was clear the painting represented no scene presently before them. Instead it showed a seashore, a deep blue ocean and a long line of white surf. On the shore was a bamboo cottage, near which stood an elephant.

Mr. Y— was aghast. "Who took my painting?" he cried. Yet it was obvious to all that the canvas had not been moved and indeed was the very one which his wet brush was then in the act of touching. The picture bore not the slightest resemblance to the view before them—a lake and a castle. It was Narayan, the personal assistant to the Prince, who broke the spell.

"Why, this is the picture of the Master's bungalow on the ocean," he said to Mr. Y—. "I did not know you had been there."

The white-faced Mr. Y— had indeed not been there, since he had come directly from Marseilles with the group. He steadfastly refused to believe he had painted the ocean scene. Yet it was clear to all others he had and that in some way the Rajput Prince had so dominated him that he saw not what was before his eyes but what the Takur wished him to see.

This is a remarkable example of complete personality domination, possible only to an adept. Yet every day we see evidence of the same process to a lesser degree. Most successful business men use this power to achieve their purposes. Psychic energy can be employed in this way to attain material ends but in a sense this is a debasement of a miraculous power that is capable of bringing you far more valuable rewards. For it is possible to use psychic energy to increase your store of psychic energy and I will tell you how to do this in the next chapter.

TWELVE

Achieving
Psychic Development

In the warm dust of a road leading into Benares sits a holy man. He is singing and his voice is surprisingly loud and clear as it lingers on the broad vowel sounds in the verses. He is chanting the ancient Upanishads, reminding the passers-by of the glory that once was India's and calling them anew to action. Of the hundreds who pass only a few take notice. They smile indulgently and place small coins at his feet. But not one heeds his summons.

You pause. You observe. You approach him. A little proud in your knowledge you ask, "Why do so few hear your call, O Holy One?"

He raises his eyes and as they meet yours, they change. The far-away look vanishes and the deep brown pupils come alive with an inner fire. There is keen intelligence and a touch of wry humor in them as he answers, "You have been called many times but do *you* follow the path of right action?"

Having spoken, his face relaxes, his eyes gaze into the distance and he resumes the sing-song Hindi chant, "Indra smote the mighty mountain, and it opened, and out of it flowed two streams of clear water."

You stand rooted to the spot, amazed at the strange experience, while the old man's words ring loudly in your mind—"Do you follow the path of right action?"

What is meant by "right action"? We live in a world of action.

Every waking minute we take some form of action, for to stop action is to die. But what is "right action"?

Every world religion, every world Teacher has endeavored to instruct in right action. This is one of the directions of the eight-fold path of Gautama Buddha. Asked by a pupil to amplify his views on right action, the Blessed One said:

> Distinguish between those who understand and those who agree. He who understands the Teaching will not tarry in applying it to life; he who agrees will nod and extol the Teaching as remarkable wisdom, but will not apply this wisdom to his life.
>
> There are many who have agreed, but they are like a withered forest, fruitless and without shade. Only decay awaits them.
>
> Those who understand are few, but like a sponge they absorb the precious knowledge and are ready to cleanse the horrors of the world with the precious liquid.

It is in the hope you will understand and seek out your own road to right action that this chapter is written. It is not for everyone to follow the same path. Each must find his own. For you to find your way to the control of your destiny and mastery of your environment, psychic energy is needed. This will guide your steps to the right road and give you the strength to follow it.

Developing Your Psychic Centers—Transformers of High-Grade Energy

There are many grades of psychic energy. At first only the lowest grades, those nearest physical energy, can be acquired and employed. But as you work with energy and gain more, your psychic centers begin to develop. These transformers, for that is what they are, then begin with ever-increasing efficiency to seine in more and more high-grade energy and make it available to you. In this chapter we will describe these centers, their purposes and how they may be developed.

In the training given to Rosicrucian students, the exercises

prescribed in Chapter Eleven and other similar exercises are practiced for two years before further instruction is given. It is assumed that certain basic controls will have been learned and
mastered during that period. While it may not be practical for
you to serve this long apprenticeship, a certain length of time
and a certain amount of effort are needed to build a solid foundation. Before proceeding much further you should, for example,
have some skill in projecting physical energy, in manipulating
physical objects without actual contact with them. You may have
already discovered that the simplest way is to talk to them. This
does not imply that an inanimate object can hear a command and
obey it. Of course not. The vocal command is an artifice designed
to focus all your attention and energy upon the desired objective.
It is very similar to a command given an animal like a dog or a
horse. You not only speak to it but you simultaneously exert an
aura of energy to reinforce your will. The words are entirely
subordinate to the focused thought reinforced by energy. Speak to
inanimate objects in the same way. Once you get over a certain
self-consciousness, you will find it easier than controlling animals.
After all, most animals have a will of their own and it may be at
odds with yours, whereas inanimate things offer no such resist-
ance.

If you have not already acquired this skill, start to learn now.
At first, practice with some object that can be moved with but a
very small amount of force. Try one of the following.

1. Suspend a weight of about one-half an ounce from a light
   thread approximately 18 inches long. Be careful not to
   breathe upon it. When it has stopped oscillating and has
   become perfectly still, command it to swing, swing like a
   pendulum or swing in a circle. Say to it "Swing!" just as
   you would say "Heel!" to a dog or "Whoa!" to a horse. Be
   sure you have the right mental attitude. When you say
   "Whoa!" to a horse you expect the command to be obeyed
   and even may feel a slight indignation if the horse does not
   obey immediately. Your attitude with the pendulum should
   be exactly the same.
2. Fill a soup plate with water and set it upon a solid table.

Stand away so your breath will not affect it and then command the water to ripple. Say "R-r-r-r-ripple" in a firm voice. It will—not much at first, but after you get the knack you will have it splashing out of the dish.

3. Lay a completely round and smooth pencil or piece of metal or plastic tubing on a level table with a smoothly varnished top. Then command the pencil to roll towards you. Say "Come here!" to it, or "Roll over here!" just as you would command a dog to "Roll over."

The foregoing exercises are simple and easy to perform but they will give you confidence. Once you understand and have confidence in your ability to exert force at a distance, you can then proceed to learn about higher psychic energy and how to employ it.

The unknown is always discovered through the known. This is the way we learn. To acquire a new skill, to learn a new technique, we must start with something simple that we already have learned and understand. From that point onward we may progress into uncharted waters but we learn by doing, not by just thinking about it.

We never get something for nothing. This means we must work for and earn the psychic development we seek. True, we have all read or heard of the "instant revelation," of Boehme the shoemaker, of Paul on the road to Damascus and countless others. These men but recalled something they already knew, a skill they had worked hard for many lives to acquire, and their memories were jarred into complete recollection by an incident. Very few today have that dormant skill waiting to be awakened. But many have already had some previous training and need but a year or two of concentrated effort to bring it to full flower. With the impatience characteristic of the times, these seekers, recalling dimly their former ability, usually look for magic formulae, secret words, odd physical postures and other devices that they hope will in a matter of hours or days bring them mastership. If they had ever achieved mastery over themselves and their environment, this knowledge and ability would be theirs forever, ready to be called into action on demand. But very few, not more than a thousand in this world of billions, have attained this eminence. The rest of us still have a lot of work ahead of us.

Exercises in Using Your Psychic Centers

There are no shortcuts. Do not be deceived by the claims and advertisements that offer instant development, quick Divine aid and magical solutions to your problems. There are none. But if you will work at your development, really work at it, you can so change your physical equipment that you will be able to do things a year or so from now that today you regard as impossible. These new powers come quite naturally as your psychic centers open and accelerate their motion. The exercises and explanations that follow are to help you bring this about.

The basic law of this Universe is that energy follows thought. Automatically and without any volition on your part, energy flows from you to wherever you direct your attention. Usually we think of material things, the world around us, other people, ourselves, and when our attention is so focused energy flows away from us and we eventually become depleted. This is why we need to sleep. The outflow of energy has to be temporarily stopped, or cut way down, and we must spend a few hours each day replacing what we have distributed.

We experience a loss of energy when we turn our attention to people or objects or situations of an equal or lower vibratory rate than our own. The law of descending energy applies. However, when we turn our attention to entities of a higher vibratory rate, we receive energy. Our line of thought, our directed attention, provides a connection or channel along which the radiations of higher energy flow to us. Thus it is well to turn your attention to the sun, or to the stars or to certain planets with high vibrating rates like Venus and Jupiter, but not to the moon or Mars or Saturn, because their radiated energies are of a lower rate than those of the Earth. Those are physical visible entities but we can also turn our attention to Great Beings that do not ordinarily manifest in physical form and from them receive a corresponding return of high-grade energy which will stimulate and rejuvenate us in every way, physical, mental and spiritual.

We can use this law, that energy follows thought, to improve ourselves. We can increase our physical and psychic energy, but more than this, we can so energize certain parts of our bodies and certain psychic centers so that they will become stronger and function more efficiently. Now I will tell you how to do this and it is my earnest hope that you will remember these suggestions and practice these exercises as long as you live.

The Heart Center

Here is the first exercise. It is designed to stimulate and rouse your heart center into action. It uses a visualization which aids you to keep your attention focused upon the psychic center in your heart.

1. Sit erect in a straight-backed chair in a dimly lit room. Shut out sound as best you can and try to prevent interruption.
2. Close your eyes and turn your attention inward toward your heart.
3. Now in imagination enter your heart. To your surprise you are now standing on a plain before a hill and on the top of the hill is a temple. Hold this visualization, for this is the temple of the heart.
4. Now climb the hill, mount the steps of the temple and enter the center doorway. Observe the appearance of the temple. Is it well kept, swept and clean? Or is it covered with dust?
5. Walk into the dimly lit interior and approach the central adytum. As you draw near you observe a flickering light within. The flame grows brighter as you approach and you can see it swell and recede rhythmically in the bowl-like depression in the center of the room.
6. Gaze upon this flame. Send it your energies. See it respond and grow bright and strong as it reaches up to touch the ceiling forty feet above. You are feeding the flame of your heart. You are stimulating it to growth. Breathe deeply and

realize in the depths of your being that your heart center is coming alive.

7. Open your eyes and sit in quiet meditation for five minutes before rising and terminating the exercise.

This is not a Hatha Yoga exercise. There should be no compression of breath in the solar plexus or heart area. Your breathing throughout should be normal but deep. The effects are achieved by the visualization, which focuses your attention in an uninterrupted fashion on the heart center and thus feeds energy into it. The additional stimulating helps this important center expand and grow strong. Perform this exercise once a week but never more than twice a week at first.

This simple visualization is given at the very beginning of these exercises because the heart center is the most important. As we proceed in this chapter the techniques offered will become increasingly complex. The initial simple visualization will proceed to color visualization, then to overlapping color, then to sound, to sound and color, and so on. The purpose of this is to provide you with the means to open your psychic centers and so enable you to bring higher psychic energies into your being and under your control. The training must proceed in stages. No one should try to run before he has learned to walk. It would be equally foolish and just as futile for you to try to by-pass the preliminaries and go right to the most sophisticated practices. Nothing would happen. Your physical apparatus cannot perform the functions required until it has been trained and developed. But if you follow the recommended sequence and remain long enough in each stage, I can promise you surprising and most gratifying results.

Let me repeat now, the heart center is the most important of all your psychic centers. For this reason it is wise to give it the most attention and strive first for its development. It is one of the two centers which are in direct connection with the Higher Self and through which soul energy and the other higher energies enter your being. The other avenue of entrance is the head center, which is located in almost the exact center of your head in the vicinity of the pineal gland. The heart center is on the left side of the spine and close to it in the vicinity of your physical heart. In fact the heart center is so close to the physical heart and the head center so close to the pineal gland that if you turn your attention to these physical organs you will, for all practical purposes, be focusing your energies in the corresponding psychic centers.

The Seven Major Psychic Centers

You have seven major psychic centers, three sacred, or higher, psychic centers, three profane, or lower, psychic centers, and the solar plexus center between them. We will not pay very much attention to the lower psychic centers, which are located in the stomach, the sex organs and at the base of the spine. In fact we are going to avoid them quite pointedly. They have already received more than their share of attention over the long years of man's development and they still get too much. Most of the problems we face today stem from the overactivity of these lower centers, which are the most highly developed and most powerful translators of energy we possess. They seize greedily upon all energy available to them and in all too many people this may run as high as 90 percent. So in order to become better balanced, we must work to bring our higher centers up to a comparable peak of efficiency. If we can succeed we will then be veritable supermen.

The training here given is thus aimed at improving our sacred centers, the head, the heart, and also the throat center which is located in the neck back of the Adam's apple. The three functioning properly become a triangle of energies which when linked together are well nigh irresistible. As each center develops it becomes more efficient in gathering and transforming ever-higher grades of energy and it also enlarges its sphere of influence. In time it contacts the other two centers, and if they have developed to the necessary degree a linkage is created. It is this triangle of interlaced and interacting high-grade energy which will enable you to perform seeming miracles, and in days to come it will provide you with a vehicle in which to live apart from your physical body.

Exercises for Developing Your Psychic Centers

The exercises for developing your psychic centers fall generally into three groups, namely those which employ sound, color and mental energy. There are many techniques in each group, all of them dependent to different degrees on visualization. I will give you two or three examples of each group and suggest you try them all, and also any others you devise for yourself. Then select the exercises that appeal most and continue them until you achieve the desired results.

Sound. The use of sound has always played an important role in psychic development. The tone, intensity and quality of certain sounds have definite effects upon people. Thunder frightens, music soothes and words persuade. Long ago it was discovered that certain combination of vowels and consonants on different notes affect not only the physical but the psychic body. The monks in the monasteries of northern India, Tibet and China sing a group of these sounds over and over. "Om mane padme humm" may be heard there at almost any hour chanted in a singsong rhythm by male voices. This is called a mantram and it is a powerful one. Unfortunately, or possibly fortunately, most of the monks who participate do not have the mental development and understanding needed to take advantage of the energy they focus upon themselves. They are well-meaning religious, nothing more. But a few here and there do understand and use the power of sounds as I will explain it to you.

In the literal sense, any uttered sound designed to achieve a human response is a mantram. The spoken word is always more persuasive than the same word written. The history of speech is long and involved, far too complicated to detail here. So I must skip a great deal of preliminary explanation and tell you that the word "mantram" is today used to describe a sound or group of sounds designed to stimulate certain physical and psychic areas in the human body.

From time immemorial sounds have been associated with ideas and the same sounds usually carry from one language to another. The sound "ah," usually represented in writing by "a," is an almost universal sound for energy. The sound of "rr," represented by "r," usually has a masculine connotation signifying control, leadership, etc. We have the many different language renditions of father, pater, fater, pere, padre as well as ruler, rex, royal, roi, Kaiser, Caesar, etc. The feminine, mothering, nourishing idea is usually represented by the "mm" sound, written "m" in most languages. Here we have mother, mutter, madre, maman, mater, and so on. When these basic sounds are uttered in certain combinations, the legacy of a thousand centuries goes to work on the emotional nature of the listener. This can be easily observed. Not so obvious, but equally effective, is the influence upon the psychic centers. Certain sounds have a more profound effect on some centers than on others and experiments over the centuries have brought this to light.

The sound "ra" (pronounced "rah"), for example, if intoned loudly and fully for nine times in succession, will bring a noticeable increase in physical energy. This is like a chant and all intonations should be on the same note, a note convenient and comfortable for your voice, such as A above middle C. The sound "ma," if intoned nine successive times on the same note and in the same manner, will produce a warm, comfortable physical feeling, a feeling of being nourished and cared for.

These sounds also have an effect upon the psychic body, somewhat in the same manner as they affect the physical. They may be used in combination in the sound "ra-ma," which gives a deeper and more profound stimulus to the psychic centers.

The sound "ra-ma" affects all the sacred psychic centers but it has its greatest effect upon the pituitary gland and the corresponding portion of the head center. This will be discussed later when we study the head center.

Another very powerful mantram is the combination A-U-M. This is usually intoned as one sound "aum" and as a rule the note of D above middle C is preferred. Like the combination "ra-ma," it has a beneficial effect on the physical body and upon all the higher psychic centers. However, it has a particularly powerful influence on the pineal gland and that portion of the head center for which it is the physical doorway. The head center is in two halves and this peculiar phenomenon will be described later in this chapter. The Rosicrucians use several other mantra but space will not permit consideration of all. We will, however, describe all the sounds and combinations of sounds found to be particularly effective in stimulating the psychic centers. Important among these are "tho," "ehm," "meh" and "err."

"*Tho*" is pronounced like "throw" without the "r." Emphasis is placed upon the "th" sound and it is carried for one-half the total duration of the entire mantram. It is usually repeated three or seven successive times and it affects the throat center and its corresponding gland, the thyroid.

"*Ehm*" is pronounced like "aim." It affects the thymus gland particularly and has a beneficial influence upon the heart center.

"*Meh*" is pronounced like "met" but with an "h" ending instead of the "t." The "h" is aspirated with emphasis as the sound is intoned, usually on middle C. This has a soothing effect on the physical nervous system and a stirring influence on the heart center.

"*Err*" is pronounced "urr" and the "rr" sound is sustained at the end. This mantram is particularly helpful in clearing an upset or chaotic condition in the mind or emotions and should be used for that purpose. Physically, the sound will often create ripples upon a glass of water. Psychically, it has the same regulating effect and will aid the advanced student control the psychic energy at his command.

There are many other mantra, some composed of single words and others of combination of words. While each is designed for a specific purpose, every one has an over-all beneficial influence.

It is safest and best to develop the heart center first. This can be done by turning your attention to your heart, by visualizing energy flowing into and surrounding the heart, by seeing that energy vibrating as a shining pink cloud (a visualization) and by intoning the various mantra that stimulate the heart center. You have been given an exercise designed to focus attention on the heart. Practice this once or twice a week preferably in the morning upon arising. On the other days in the week perform one or more of the following exercises.

Mantram. Sit comfortably with your feet flat on the floor, your spine straight and your head erect.

Intone softly but quite audibly the following mantram seven times consecutively without pausing. Do not vary the tone.

RA-MEH-RA-MA-RA-MEH.

Color plus mantram. Sit as indicated before. Visualize a pink cloud around your body at the level of the heart. See the cloud pulsate in rhythm with your heart's beat. Intone softly.

U-U-U-U-U-U-UMM.

The "U" is pronounced "ooh."

Do this three times. The intonations should coincide with the visualization of the pink cloud.

Energy flow. Sit as indicated. Visualize a white cloud of vibrant energy over your head. The cloud should be very white, like sunlight on newly fallen snow. Know that this cloud is composed of vital primary energy of the highest sort. Then, by an act of the will, bring the cloud down into your heart, entering the body at the left of the spinal column between the shoulder blades.

These exercises will bring a great stimulus of energy to your heart center and if you do nothing to dissipate, block off or lower this energy in between times, you will find after about two months that certain changes are taking place within you. Do not make the mistake of dissipating this precious heart energy on unworthy projects such as romantic affairs or fanatical pursuits, and do not block it off by indulging in vanity or any form of tempestuousness. If you permit it to help you as it can and will, you will find you are able to understand others better, you will catch their moods and sometimes read their thoughts. This will make you more understanding, tolerant and compassionate, essential requirements before you can safely develop your other sacred centers. When it becomes obvious to you that the person with you at the moment is sad or excited or depressed or joyful, and when you know in advance what they intend to say to you, this is an indication that your heart center is becoming active and you may then go on to the exercises for other centers. This obviously does not refer to someone close to you with whom you already have established an attunement, but to a more casual encounter. When things you have not witnessed but have only read or heard about impress you deeply and you become concerned for the welfare of the persons involved, this is also a sign of a developing heart center.

The Head Center

As has been mentioned, the head center in the average human is in two parts. One half animates the physical brain and is in close connection with all your physical equipment. It is the awareness area of your being for every physical sensation, every physical action and all of your stored memories and skills. The pituitary gland is the physical organ which is the point of transfer for impressions and ideas in this half of your head center. As you know, the pituitary is a very small, shapeless organ about one-eighth inch in diameter located in the head about one inch behind the root of the nose between the eyes.

Near to the pituitary gland and behind it, almost in the exact center of your head is the pineal gland. This is also a small organ, of fleshy consistency, not much larger than the pituitary. The pineal gland is not connected with the pituitary and in fact is separated from it by what appears to be heavy cartilaginous tissue. The pineal is aligned with the higher half of your head center and is one of the two points in your physical body which is in contact with the soul and where the soul energy enters your body. The other is, as you know, the heart center. The soul, your higher self, is fully aware of all that you think and do and of all the impressions that come to you. But since your conscious awareness is focused in the physical brain, as is that of every other person, and since the physical brain and its psychic counterpart, the lower half of the head center, are separated from the higher, you do not partake consciously of the energies and knowledge which your soul and higher self possess. But as the two halves of the head center develop, they grow larger. Finally they make contact and an avenue of communication is set up between them, even though the upper half vibrates at a faster rate than the lower. This connecting link is called the antahkarana or psychic bridge. At first this pathway is small and only a limited communication is possible. But even so this will bring inspiration and some intuitive flashes to your consciousness focused in the lower half. As your efforts continue and the antahkarana is enlarged and strengthened, your intuitive powers will grow and your understanding broaden accordingly.

Let me make it quite clear that this "break-through" in the separation between the higher and lower halves of the head center is in no wise a cutting through or puncturing of physical bone or tissue. The channel or bridge that is created is entirely in the psychic areas, not the physical.

As the heart center shows signs of becoming active, continue its training regime but now add to this some or all of the following exercises for the head center. To stimulate the pituitary and expand the lower portion of the head center, these are recommended.

Mantram. Sound RA-MA seven times. Pause. Repeat seven times. Pause. Repeat nine times. This is to be done while sitting erect. The inhalation should be quick and deep. The sound is carried out on the prolonged exhalation. Be sure to maintain a tautened muscular structure in your erect spine and keep your muscular corset solid throughout the exercise. This, interestingly, allows the psychic centers to become more active, particularly the all-important heart center.

Color plus mantram. Visualize a bright yellow slightly tinged with green, like sunlight falling through the leaves of trees, while sounding the following mantram three times:

RA-RA-RA, MA-MA-MA.

RA-A-A—MA-A-A.

Energy flow. Visualize the same sunlight yellow and, while directing the color to the area of the pituitary gland in the forefront of the head between your eyes, silently intone three times: RA-A-A, MA-A-A.

It is important that these exercises for the pituitary gland and the lower half of the head center be started well before any attempt is made to develop the higher head center. Likewise, it should be noted here again that a substantial effort should be made with the heart center before any attention is given to either the head centers or the throat center.

The first noticeable effect of the pituitary exercises will be an increase in your powers of observation, a speeding up in your thinking process and an improvement in your memory. When this is observed, then start the following exercise designed to stimulate the pineal gland and awaken the higher head center. Meanwhile continue the heart and lower head center exercises, or those of them that seem to give you the most satisfaction and the best results. For the present I suggest now only one exercise for the higher mind. You will note it is a combination of all techniques offered.

Exercise. Sit erect as previously indicated. Focus your attention on the pineal gland, which is situated in the center of your head at the level of your ears. It is behind and slightly lower than the pituitary. Visualize a violet color shading towards the pink and see this energy envelop the pineal gland in a sort of haze. Then sound the mantram AUM seven times. Pause. Then repeat seven times. Pause. Then again seven times. The first and last series should be pronounced audibly, preferably in full voice. If the sound volume presents a problem, intone it softly but still audibly. The second series should be intoned silently. When this silent chanting is properly employed it is more effective than the audible intonation in stimulating the pineal area. So study it. The audible intonation of AUM should end in a sustained humming sound. Locate the vibrations of this sound in the pineal gland. Feel them massage the gland until it responds with a similar vibratory action, almost as if it were glowing with that same violet-pink color. Practice this series, audible, silent, audible, twice a day, preferably early morning and just before retiring each day. Continue this several weeks before attempting the next series.

The Throat Center

Before commenting further on the development of the head center—and there is much to be said—I wish you to spend some time on developing your throat center and give you now an exercise which is designed to do this. As you have been told, the throat center is located just forward of the spinal column immediately behind the Adam's apple and is associated with the thyroid gland. Thus when working to develop this center your attention should be focused on the thyroid.

> *Exercise.* Sit in the usual erect position and, after turning your attention to the thyroid, visualize it surrounded by a bright orange light and at the same time intone the following mantram in full voice:
> THO-THO-RAMA-THO.
> Intone "THO" on F sharp above middle C and "RAMA" on A natural above middle C. This interesting short chant should be repeated five times. Practice this once a day, beginning about two weeks after you start the exercise to stimulate the pineal gland and from that time onward performing them together one after the other. The sequence is not important but the amount of thought and focused attention you put into these simple techniques is very important. Your progress will depend upon it.

You are now working toward a higher psychic development. Gradually at first and then more rapidly you will change. You will become aware of the thoughts of others. At first you will regard them as your own and not realize you are picking up a signal from without. As the experience is repeated you will be able to detect which of them originate with you and which come from the mind of another. There may come a day when you will hear a voice call your name and speak to you distinctly while you are quite alone. This means your progress has been observed and you have reached a degree of advancement where you may qualify for the higher spiritual training which is given telepathically, training for Hierarchical initiation.

From a psychological point of reference, this means that your three higher centers are starting to function and an attunement between them is developing. It means, too, that the two halves of your head center are coalescing into a unit. Now it is possible to speed up the attunement between the heart, head and throat centers, and you will find the following exercises a great help.

Exercise

Part one. Sit as usual with your head erect and your back straight. Focus your attention in your heart center and as you do so, see it bathed in a pink cloud.

Inhale to the count of seven. Hold the breath in for the count of ten, and as you do so turn your attention to your higher head center. Take the pink cloud along and see it enclose the higher head center within itself.

Then breathe out to the count of seven, meanwhile keeping your attention at the top of your head.

Finally, hold your breath out of your lungs for the count of ten and as you do so see the pink cloud expand and embrace your entire body.

Part two. Next, focus your attention on your throat center and see it bathed in a blue light, like blue sky on a clear day. Inhale to the count of seven.

Then turn your attention to your higher head center and see the blue cloud envelop it as you count to ten.

Hold the cloud in place as you exhale to the count of seven.

Then hold the breath out of your lungs for a count of ten, while the blue cloud enlarges and envelopes your whole body.

Part three. Now focus your attention in your lower head center and see a brilliant white light surround your pituitary gland as you inhale to the count of seven.

Hold your breath for the count of ten and see the white cloud embrace both the pituitary and pineal gland areas as you bring these two glands into alignment in your mind's eye.

Then release your breath to the count of seven but hold your now-completed head center in the center of the brilliant white light.

Finally, hold your breath out for the count of ten and as you do so see the white light expand until it encloses your whole body and extends all around you to a distance of two or three feet.

Sound AUM three times and then arise, putting all thought of the exercise out of your mind immediately.

This is a most powerful exercise and, as you observe, it is designed to stimulate all three sacred centers and to create an attunement among them. In order for it to be effective you must build up to it gradually. Do not make the mistake of attempting it before you have achieved at least a partial development of the individual centers. No harm will befall you if you do, but no good will be accomplished either.

You will now notice a difference in yourself, a vast difference. Each new thought will transfix you like an arrow. You will be aware of a new inner vibration almost as if there were a flame inside you. At intervals when alone you will hear the voice of an instructor and later as you build ever-higher energies into your being you will have flashes of Cosmic Consciousness, that state in which you are able to contact all knowledge. Thus will develop in you the ability to contact the wondrous, perilous, subtlest energies, those that transform life and confute the concept of death. You will need less and less sleep, yet your energy will in no way diminish—on the contrary it will appear to be limitless. Your breath will be easier, you will breathe more deeply and freely even at high altitudes and the pathway to the astral world will open up before you, if you want it to.

Now your knowledge will increase rapidly but you will regard it as insignificant. People will laud you and attempt to bestow distinctions upon you, but they will mean but little and you will accept them graciously only because you are unwilling to risk hurting their feelings. The standard organized religions will hold less and less interest for you and their contentions with each other will seem to you like quarrels of children. Your earthly lineage, whether it be highest or lowest, will no longer have any importance to you, since you will now be consciously aware of the brotherhood of men. You will lose all capacity for harsh and unkind words, you will cheerfully repeat your tasks many times if circumstances require it and you will harbor no resentment against those who make them difficult. Your heart and mind will be filled with a striving toward an ever-clearer vision, toward an ever-broader understanding, and as you gain great power you will grow equally in humility. Truly you will have changed!

The training program given in this chapter is designed solely for the development of your higher centers but, you must realize, the energy you draw to yourself will tend to follow the law of descending energy and trickle down into your solar plexus center and your lower centers if you permit it. It all rests with you and where you focus your attention. Being human, it is inevitable that your interests, desires and habits will receive a certain amount of your time and attention. These thoughts, emotions and actions all require energy and there is no question but that a certain percentage of the new energy will be so employed and its vibratory rate lowered in the process. Until you reach a higher stage of development and your control improves, you will not be able to prevent this. Many times you will not even want to, but will take pride and pleasure in the additional stimulus your physical nature receives.

This will, of course, lengthen the period of your development and make its attainment more difficult. Many fascinating by-roads will open up and tempt you. The lower appetites, for example, will demand more and more attention. Sex, food, drink, leisure and luxury will become more appealing and make greater demands on your self-control. You think now these are obvious pitfalls which can be easily avoided but when the time comes that you must face them, you will be amazed and often confused by the strange and subtle approaches you encounter. Since this has all been well documented by hundreds of mystics, you should not have too much difficulty in finding and following the proper narrow path through these temptations.

Once this stage has been met and conquered, many students feel they are well along on the road to higher development and that it will only be a question of days or weeks before they will be admitted into the Ashram of a Master. But if acquiring self-control is difficult, the next test, that of learning discrimination, is even more so. Because it is at this point that your psychic centers start to open and, as a rule, the very first door to open is through the solar plexus center. This path leads only to glamor and illusion, and if you follow it you will become hopelessly lost. The opening solar plexus center awakens the lower psychic faculties, which means that you gradually become aware of all sorts of beings, sights, sounds and smells which exist on the astral plane. Here are the astral bodies of people recently dead and even some who have been dead a long time. Here are entities which have never had carnal existence but are the creations of human emotion and thought. Here can be found various sizes and shapes of animal-like entities, some like the animals of our physical world, others like nothing you have ever seen. More often than not, this is the realm contacted by visionaries, seers, psychics and the average spiritualistic seance, a world whose inhabitants are no more dependable or wiser than the average man you might meet on the street, and often far more fallible.

As your solar plexus center becomes active you will hear voices and see forms which cannot be apprehended by the physical senses. Most often they will be vague as to outline of figure and blurred as to clarity of speech. These are the telltale characteristics of the astral world, the unfinished sentences, the attempts to terrify, the efforts to stimulate an emotional response, and beings with an ordinary appearance, no beauty, no radiance. Yet many on the road to development are impressed by what they see and what they are told in this environment. Do not permit yourself to be thus ensnared. Clairvoyance and clairaudience are natural by-products which come as a result of higher psychic development. When they are sought as ends in themselves before that development has been achieved, they can be attained but they are then not reliable. The illusory seems real and the desire to see and hear more and more leads to acceptance of the greatest deceptions. Then discrimination is cast aside and satisfaction is sought in parading dubious observations before your gaping and credulous fellow creatures.

At this point you must again apply self-discipline. Pride and vanity will lead you into great error, if you will permit them. But they can be excised by the scalpel of the intellect. Maintain your balance and the ability to discriminate between the true and the false, between the real and the unreal. The bell-like tones of your Teacher in your inner ear, once heard, will ever stand apart and above the blurred reports of your lower psychic faculties.

The best answer is to work diligently to develop your heart and head centers. As they open, your vision will clear and you will see the astral illusion for what it is. Other dimensions will open before you, enabling you to turn with ease from paralyzing self-interest to the freedom of true brotherly love. The motives of others will become clear and in knowing them, you will be able to forgive even the worst transgressions. A feeling for events will also grow in you and will enable you to appraise sensitively the values in each situation you encounter. Not the least of the gifts of this growth are compassion for others and a reluctance to take any step which will hurt them.

To a student who asked how he might attain to Cosmic attunement, his Teacher replied,

> Purify your thoughts and after determining your three worst defects, sacrifice them on the altar of your striving. Strengthen your body and its centers by proper breathing and proper thought, as prescribed. Then you will behold the stars of the spirit; you will see the flames of the purification of the centers; you will hear the voice of the invisible Teacher and you will acquire those subtle perceptions which will transform your life.

And then he added,

> You will not return to the old shore of the stream, for you will have realized that joy is a special wisdom. You will not live apart from life but you will enter it unnoticeably, without human distinctions. You will observe, but you will not court attention. Evolution is not wrought by crowds and the current of space you have entered will guard you against the arrows of the crowd's attention. This does not mean that

there is needed even the slightest alienation from your normal life. It is only necessary to estimate and measure the goal-fitness of the things which surround you.

Only a few have the ability to achieve illumination but everyone, by striving, can approach and embrace her two younger sisters, inspiration and intuition. These teachings are useful for all. They will sustain health, reinforce memory and purify thoughts.

THIRTEEN

The Secret of
Psychic Projection

For many hundreds of years the Rosicrucians have taught the secret of psychic projection. There are many types and many levels of projection but to the new student the Rosicrucians generalize them all under the term "psychic projection."

Astral Projection

Today we hear often about astral projection. This is a fairly common form of involuntary projection which usually happens without plan and often without the projecting person being aware of the near-miracle he has accomplished. There are literally thousands of recorded instances, all of them well authenticated. You yourself may have experienced this phenomenon. It most often is the result of a powerful emotional surge toward a loved one, either to protect or to ask for aid. The woman in distress who cries out to her husband, who hears her though he is hundreds of miles away; the parent who tries to warn an absent son and captures his attention in time to save him from danger—these are classic examples. In these situations a common bond of love or mutual understanding acts as the pathway, or conducting medium, along which the message flows, driven by a most powerful emotional surge in order to break through into the conscious awareness of the receiver. The physical senses are not involved and the entire transmission takes place on the emotional or astral level.

This is one of several kinds of projection. There are also etheric projection, mental projection and soul projection. All are on different vibratory levels; some are consciously controlled and others are not. The Rosicrucians are interested only in controlled projection. They teach you how you may project at will and also how to make the person you are trying to reach aware of your presence. This is best achieved through etheric projection, which I will explain to you in this chapter. But first I wish to make clear to you exactly what is to be accomplished. So let us look at one or two well-known examples of projection.

Two Examples of Etheric Projection

The first is the case of Monsignor Alphonsus Ligouri, Abbott of the monastery at Arienzo in Italy. On the morning of September 21, 1774, Father Ligouri was found in what appeared to be a deep sleep. This was a matter of some concern to his brother monks because he was scheduled to be the celebrant at mass that morning and had never before been late for his duty. All efforts to rouse him failed but his heart was regular, though the beat was slow, and his breathing seemed easy enough, so aside from putting him in a comfortable position and placing a coverlet over him, no particular treatment was accorded him.

When he awoke twelve hours later, several of his brother monks were in the room and he asked them "Why are you all standing here?"

"We have been worried about you," was the reply. "You haven't moved for hours and we thought you were dying. We were here praying for you."

Ligouri then said something very strange. "I am all right, but I have just been in Rome, where I stood at the bedside of the Pope, who is now dead."

His listeners assumed he had been dreaming, for Rome was four days journey from Arienzo, but four days later, when word came from Rome, they were astonished to learn that the Pope had indeed died at the time when Monsignor Ligouri was in the trance-like sleep. And more than that, among those seen in attendance at the bedside of the dying Pontiff had been Alphonsus Ligouri.

Other details soon came to light. Everyone who was present, including the superiors of the Dominican, Observatine and Augustinian Orders, not only spoke to Ligouri but joined him as he led the prayers for the dying Pope. Here, therefore, were two sets of witnesses who saw Ligouri both in Arienzo in a coma-like sleep, and simultaneously in Rome, some four days' journey from Arienzo. Both groups were honestly convinced that they saw Ligouri and that he had been with them.

This is known as bi-location, being in two or more places at once, and there are many such cases on record. Most of these cases are amply testified to by competent witnesses and carefully recorded. We have them in the logs of ships, in military reports and in the annals of business, as well as in the records of religion. Of course, in religious records we find the most striking examples, among which the multi-appearances of Milarepa at the time of his death is noteworthy. This great Tibetan mystic and saint had taught all over India and Ceylon, as well as in Tibet. At the time of his death, knowing that his transition was expected and had been foretold, his disciples and followers, of which there were many thousands, had gathered together in groups to pray. There were literally hundreds of these groups scattered all over southern Asia, from the mountains of Tibet through Afghanistan, India and Burma right down into Ceylon and the Malay states. On the day of his death, Milarepa was seen in physical form by every one of these groups. Each group, each person in each group, was convinced he had seen and touched Milarepa in the flesh and each thought their group was the only one so honored.

How to Achieve Etheric Projection

In these two striking examples we have seen etheric projection effectively accomplished by the impressive power of thought. This seems contrary to all reason, yet it can be done. Now, I propose to tell you how. This skill like any other skill must be attained *through practice.* An accomplished pianist can explain how to play the piano and even demonstrate it, but you will never bring music out of the instrument yourself until you have acquired the necessary technique. Projection requires similar training.

First we will start with an exercise in mental projection. We choose this not because it is easier. Actually, competent mental projection is more difficult than etheric projection, but it will be easier to understand at first. Etheric projection *seems* impossible to you and everyone else who has not experienced it, so you will in consequence have a great many mental blocks against it. But it is not too difficult to imagine traveling in your mind to a distant spot, so that is how we will begin.

Preparation

1. Do not attempt this when you are physically exhausted, or have just finished eating or at any other time when the blood is likely to be drawn from the head to other parts of the body. This is important. Your mind must be clear and active, not cluttered and somnolent. Thus, a full complement of blood in the brain is necessary.

2. Take a bath and cleanse yourself thoroughly, including your mouth and teeth. In a word, remove from yourself as much extraneous physical matter as you can. Usually a shower is better than a tub. This cleansing process is quite important, so do not neglect it. It has both a practical and a psychological effect, practical in that it will free you from both material and astral contamination, psychological in that you will actually feel mentally and emotionally cleaner.

3. Put on a light garment, a nightdress or a set of pajamas or a single clean robe.

4. Select a place where you will not be interrupted, a place which is also as quiet as it is possible to find.

5. Sit in a comfortable chair with a back high enough to rest your head, or lie flat on a bed or couch. A large arm chair is better, as a rule, because it is easier to maintain awareness in a sitting position. We are all too prone to fall asleep when lying down.

Practice

1. When comfortable and relaxed, take seven deep breaths. These should be even breaths spaced in a rhythmic fashion. Inhale to the count of four, hold the breath to the count of eleven, then exhale to the count of seven. The counting should be even and regular, never hurried, never too slow.
2. When the breathing has been completed, close your eyes and visualize the place to which you wish to project. It may be the next room or it may be 1,000 miles away; it doesn't matter. But it is important that you know this place, that you have been there and are familiar with it in all its details. Then see yourself in this place. Imagine that you are in this spot you have selected. In order to do this successfully you must shut out awareness of your present physical surroundings, shut out all sights and sounds, and see in your mind's eye the appearance of the place you wish to visit. Endow this picture with every detail it is possible for you to recall, the colors, the lighting, the arrangement of objects, the characteristic sounds, the smells, all that you would be aware of if you were physically there.
3. When you can actually visualize yourself in the place selected, look about. Observe furniture arrangements, people who may be present, how they are dressed, listen to what is said. Then return your attention to your body seated in the chair or lying on the couch.
4. It is important that you retain full conscious awareness throughout. Do not fall into a dream state. There will be a strong inclination to do so but you must resist it. The moment you slide into a dream state, you have a tendency to become an actor on the stage and not a spectator in the audience. Good projection depends upon your ability to control yourself. The dream state brings illusion and unreality. Therefore, *stay awake.*

Review

When you open your eyes back in your room, write down the exact hour and all that you observed. Later you may have an opportunity to verify your observations. This is the proper scientific approach, the attitude always encouraged by the Rosicrucians. Try, then test. Try again and test again. And again.

Success in projection presupposes certain preliminary training which most of you already have had. You must have developed the ability to concentrate, that is to shut out thoughts extraneous to the idea that you hold uppermost in your mind. In the present instance, for example, you should be able to shut out an awareness of your physical surroundings or at least dim it down while you make vivid the place you intend to visit. Then you must be able to hold that picture quite clearly and not have it blurred by other images.

Let us say you are in the bedroom of your home in New York City. You close the windows to dim down the noise outside and, after the preparation described, you put out the light and seat yourself with your eyes closed. You decide you want to visit your sister's home in rural California. You have been there and can visualize the house and the grounds around it. You do so. Now observe—is the sun out or is it cloudy? Is there a wind blowing? Do the trees move? Is there a scent from flowers? Are there people present? Who are they? How are they dressed? And so on.

It is usually that at this point the inexperienced observer gets carried away from conscious observation into a dream state. The things you did the last time you were in this house come tumbling back into your mind. You remember what was said and who was there and in a fraction of a second you are living over in recollection the events of that day long past. In other words, you will have lost control and slipped into a dream state.

Do not be discouraged. This may happen many times before you finally achieve the skill and control necessary to prevent it. So try again. Select another place to visit and start over. At first, do not spend more than fifteen minutes in projecting or trying to project. After the experience of twenty sessions this could be lengthened to a half hour but not longer. It is difficult to maintain rigid control for fifteen minutes. This requires great discipline which takes time and practice to develop, and you are to be congratulated if at first you achieve control for two or three minutes before drifting off into dreamworld.

A woman reported the following:

> I decided to project to my daughter's home and after visualizing the house which I knew well, I saw her with her two children at a table eating. I was surprised because it was mid-afternoon. But when I telephoned her later she confirmed what I had seen and said they had been having a party for the little girl, celebrating her promotion to first grade from kindergarten.

The daughter was in no way aware of her mother's observation A member in Philadelphia offered this experience:

> I was anxious to reach my wife in order to learn if she would come into the city for dinner that night or if she expected me to go home. I tried to reach her by telephone but there was no answer. It was then I thought to project to her, so I washed my hands and face and closed my office door. After quieting my nerves and mind by the regular breathing, I mentally projected to Miriam. Almost immediately I saw her. She was seated in a railroad train wearing a gray tweed suit and a black hat. I concluded she was coming to meet me in the city, and so waited for her in the office. Sure enough, she arrived about 5:30, dressed in a gray tweed suit and a black hat which was new to me, since she had bought it only that morning.

To skeptics the technique here sounds all too simple. They just can't believe it will work and their very unbelief will act as a barrier. But with an open mind, results similar to those described can be achieved with only a modest degree of training and practice. For, you see, this is a natural human ability which is within the grasp of every intelligent person. There is nothing mysterious or occult about it. All it needs to be awakened is understanding and effort. Just try it and see for yourself.

After you have had success with mental projection and begin to get the "feel of it," you can experiment with etheric projection. In etheric projection your sense of awareness is more acute.

The impacts of sight and sound and smell and even touch are much more solid than in mental projection, often almost as solid and real as they are to the senses of the physical body. This is because the etheric body is just one grade finer than the physical, but of lower vibratory rate than the mental. It possesses senses that correspond to the five physical senses and is of such quality that projections in the etheric body can often be seen, or heard, or realized in other ways by the physical senses of another. It was the etheric double of Alphonsus Ligouri that was seen and heard in Rome at the bedside of the Pope. Thus, if you would move physical matter at a distance or have someone realize your presence, you must activate and employ your etheric body.

The technique of etheric projection is different from that required in mental projection. At first it is more difficult, particularly the first two or three times you attempt to separate in full consciousness from the physical. But after you have acquired familiarity with the process and the idea is more acceptable to you, it is actually easier than good mental projection. There is no mumbo-jumbo to it. The capacity is inherent in every intelligent person and the necessary skill can be acquired with practice. It is like learning to swim. Just as in swimming, where one must learn to balance between the water and air, exerting just so much but not too much pressure upon the water in order to keep afloat, so in etheric projection one must learn to establish and maintain the same balance in a sea of energies. There is a knack to it which can be learned only through repeated experiment and practice.

The most significant difference between mental and etheric projection lies in the focus of consciousness. In mental projection you are always dimly aware of your body and what is taking place in its vicinity. Even though you may mentally be far away observing a scence of mountain and ocean, even though you may hear the dissonant tinkling of bells as a herd of goats feeds nearby in the bright sunshine, you are still conscious of the fact you are sitting in a darkened room and a truck is rumbling by on the city street outside. It is almost as if your mind is divided into two sets of awareness and you find it possible to switch your attention instantaneously from one to the other.

Etheric projection is substantially different in that when you leave the body you take all of your sensory equipment and your consciousness along with you. Your body lies as if in a coma or deep sleep and is aware of nothing until you return to it. The impressions which reach your etheric body are much more vital and just as vivid, powerful and real as physical impressions.

Before describing the technique of etheric projection and the exercises preliminary to acquiring this technique, I feel I should offer a word of caution. There are some who may regard this unusual ability as an opportunity to spy on a person or to perform some other illegal or immoral act. Now, at the very start, they must be told they will find this impossible. If you are so minded, give up the idea. Your efforts will be in vain. The very nature of etheric projection prohibits any act of which your own moral sense does not approve. You will understand as you progress how necessary to successful projection is a raising of your vibratory rate, which any of the lower emotions automatically lowers. A student describes such an incident: "I had successfully left my body and was standing in my bedroom next to the bed upon which my body lay in apparent sleep. In considering my next move I thought I would visit my sweetheart, who I suspected was entertaining a rival of mine. I experienced a pang of jealousy at the thought and without warning suddenly found myself back in my body. Nor could any amount of trying free me from it again that evening."

In this case the high tension which the young man had established with considerable effort was broken in an instant by the intrusion of a lower emotion, jealousy. Even if no jealousy had been felt, the tension would have collapsed later when he realized his visit to his sweetheart was not prompted by love but by suspicion. Now, let us proceed.

Preparation

1. Good health is a prime requisite. If you have any illness, even a minor one like a cold in the head, do not attempt etheric projection. There is a close affinity between physical and emotional imbalance. Just as an upset emotional condition will cause a deterioration in physical health, in

the same manner will physical illness affect your emotions. For successful projection your mind and emotions must be serene and calm. It is both painful and self-defeating to try to move through an emotional maelstrom deprived of the solid protection of your physical body. So do not attempt projection unless you are in good physical health.

2. As advised in mental projection, do not attempt etheric projection when physically exhausted, or immediately after eating, or at any time when the blood is likely to be drawn away from the brain to another part of the body. Also, and this is important, do not drink any alcoholic beverage for at least 48 hours prior to the experiment. This is to make sure all alcoholic influence is out of the bloodstream.

3. It must constantly be borne in mind that this is a serious experiment and not a game or a frivolous pastime. In olden times and right up to the present century, no student was permitted to attempt projection until he had trained himself for several years. Much of this preparation was in conditioning the mind to accept without cringing the shock which inevitably occurs when you first find yourself separated into two parts, so to speak, and in full possession of all your faculties. Be warned, your reaction to this experience is bound to be violent and you must be prepared for it; otherwise you will instantly return to the physical body.

4. As has already been indicated, calmness is essential. As in the preparation for mental projection, take a bath and cleanse yourself of all extraneous physical matter. With the washing, hold the thought in your mind that all of your fears and worries are also being washed from you. Make a deliberate effort to become serene and calm as you make your final preparation.

5. For this exercise it is essential you lie down, so put on a clean garment and lie on or in a bed.

Practice

1. Successful etheric projection can be accomplished only by raising your over-all vibratory rate. That is the key. Most students invariably ask, "How is this done?" There are a great number of different ways to do this, some of which

have already been explained to you. But it might be well to keep in mind the following.

a. Try to live as peaceful a life as you possibly can. This means your day-in and day-out living—not just a feeling of peace before you start the experiment, although that is of course essential.

b. Practice meditation for at least 15 minutes each day. In each meditation period make a conscious effort to raise the vibratory level of your entire being—physical, emotional and mental.

c. If you do not understand meditative techniques, prayer is an excellent substitute. Pray to God or the Cosmic to purify your nature. You must really mean this. It cannot be just lip service.

d. Set in your mind an objective, a worthwhile reason for your attempt to project etherically. Your subconscious control will not permit success in this experiment if your purpose is frivolous or selfish or ignoble. Of course, your subconscious is not unreasonable. It knows you and your limitations very well. So set a goal which is attainable and not selfish. It is all right to want to know more, to want to encounter the new and strange experiences projection will make possible. This is an acceptable goal. And it is all right to wish to become more spiritualized if you feel the experience will lead to this—as indeed it will.

e. The point in the foregoing is that the average person's reason for attempting projection is to attain some material benefit. Now there is nothing wrong in desiring material benefit, but you have to go about getting it in another way. Successful etheric projection can be accomplished only by raising your sights to higher objectives, and this automatically excludes the usual everyday benefits which are almost always associated with physical comfort and the satisfaction of the physical appetites.

2. When comfortably lying on a bed or couch, close your eyes and raise your consciousness to a point at the top of your head. Gradually your awareness of the bed beneath you and the coverlet over you, of sounds outside, of odors and air currents, should fade away and your entire con-

sciousness should be concentrated at or above the crown
of your head.

3. At this moment, intone softly and rhythmically the sound
   "OM" seven times on the note D natural above middle
   C. (A little practice beforehand will engrave this sound
   in your memory at its proper pitch.)

4. Immediately thereafter, repeat this same intonation
   silently in your head seven times. You should then be
   aware of a resonance inside your head.

5. Concentrating all of your attention on the core of this
   resonance, let it lift slowly upward toward the ceiling.
   Remember, it is the resonance that ascends, not your body.

6. Then open your eyes and allow your awareness of things
   about you to return. Do not be alarmed when you realize
   that you are no longer on the bed but above it near the
   ceiling. Above all, do not feel shock and fear when you
   observe your body, seemingly lifeless on the bed below.

7. Having demonstrated your ability to perform this experiment, return immediately to your body. This is quite
   simple and is accomplished by merely wishing to do so
   or by visualizing yourself returning to the bed and lying
   down upon it in the space your body occupies.

Results

Do not be alarmed. This is a natural process. There is
nothing supernatural or occult about it. However, the vast
majority of students experience a certain sense of shock when
they discover themselves "out of the body" and this causes an
instantaneous return to the body, somewhat in the nature of
dropping into it, which is temporarily painful and should be
avoided if possible.

If your preparation has been thorough, you could very
well succeed on your first try. Remember, though, that you
are actually turning your senses of awareness over to a body
which corresponds in all ways to your physical body, except
that it is made up of much finer material than the physical.
This etheric body has five senses—sight, hearing, taste, touch
and smell—which correspond in every way to your normal
physical senses. This exercise requires you to switch your
focus of awareness from the physical to the etheric. Since
this etheric body is made up of finer grades of matter which

are vibrating at much higher rates than physical matter, it will reflect and accept only those impacts upon it which normally will excite or stimulate these higher vibratory rates. Thus the prospects of eating a well-cooked steak washed down with a glass of beer makes no impression upon it—and if you turn your attention to this or a similar earthly attraction you will automatically flip right back into the physical. In other words you will have turned your attention to a physical-material object and to comprehend, react to, or assimilate it you must use your physical equipment, your physical body.

So if you do not have success on your first try, remember this. Try to overcome your egocentric inclinations by becoming more moderate in every way, by controlling your lower instincts and tendencies and by giving yourself over to more generous actions and to nobler desires and thoughts. Each person is a composite of millions of tiny intelligent cells, little lives so to speak, and each of these has an impulse of its own. They live on the energy which you provide but if permitted they will use this for their own purpose instead of the general good. They are responsible for all of your lower physical drives and appetites and will fight vigorously any attempt to deprive them of energy by your directing it to higher levels. Thus you must be prepared to encounter not only occasional lack of success but the feelings of inertia and discouragement which will attack you. This is just your physical body's way of saying, "Pay more attention to me and what I want, and less to these aspirations of your higher nature."

When you first find yourself out of your physical body there is no doubt that you will be surprised. The experience is quite different from what you may have anticipated. You will see and hear but until you adjust yourself to this new environment, you will not be able to touch anything. Your hand will go right through it. Walls and closed doors will offer no obstacle to your passage, nor will distance. Only after you have spent some time in your etheric vehicle and have adjusted yourself to it will you be able to use it with any degree of competence. Perhaps some reports from experimenters will help make this clearer to you.

A. L. says:

When I found myself out of my body for the first time, I was so shocked that I almost plunged right back into it again. But catching myself in time, I remembered my instructions and concentrated my attention upon the plan I had decided upon before beginning the experiment. Instantly and without any intervening sensation of motion or traveling I found myself standing in the large rotunda of Grand Central Station in New York City. No one paid the slightest attention to me and when I looked to examine myself, I saw not a body but only a vague blur of luminous matter which was almost completely transparent. This so shocked me that I returned with equal speed to my body and sat up in bed in full possession of the physical vehicle once again.

M. A. Z. reports:

I found myself out of the body near the ceiling. I turned toward the bed and when I saw myself lying there so cold and still, I thought I had died. This shocked me so much that I snapped back into the physical in the instant and this shook me up a bit, so that I hesitated for more than a week before trying again.

From R. L. we have the following:

My first four attempts were failures, so that even though I received an encouraging letter, I really did not expect to succeed on my next try. When I opened my eyes I thought I was still lying in the bed but somehow the room looked different. Then I realized that I was literally lying on the ceiling looking down at the floor. To my right I saw the bed with my body on it, eyes closed. At first I thought it was someone else and wondered who the old woman was who had come into my room. By the time I realized I was looking at myself, I was beginning to be adjusted to the new condition, so my main reaction was one of surprise to see how old and rumpled I looked, quite a bit different from my conception of my appearance. I decided to go to the next room where my daughter slept, so I moved down from the ceiling to the door. To my dismay I couldn't get the door to open but in a moment or two I discovered that by continuing on I could pass right through it.

My daughter was in her bed, sound asleep. I thought then how interesting it would be to speak to her but no matter how loudly I called, or tried to, she slept on. Then I thought I will take one of her shoes back with me to prove to her I have been there but somehow I could not pick it up. I was just beginning to feel exasperated when I found myself back in my own room, lying on the bed in the old physical shell once again.

The foregoing experiences of three people will give you some idea of what you may expect to experience when you leave the physical body for the first time. As you practice and become more skillful you will come to realize there are different vibratory levels and that you can move from one to the other by raising or lowering the vibratory rate of your etheric vehicle.

One experimenter reported that after repeated efforts he was successful in lowering his vibrations to a point where he could no longer pass through the wall of the room. Every solid object presented a barrier, just as in the physical state. In this condition his etheric form was faintly visible to ordinary physical sight and he was seen by many people. After observing that most of them were frightened he became more careful, and would present himself only before those who knew what he was doing and expected him. He found also that while in this lowered state he could move small and light physical objects. However, when in the presence of certain people (in their physical bodies) who were willing to lend their energies, he found he could move quite heavy objects with relative ease. Thinking on this, it seemed to him that this is apparently the manner in which poltergeist phenomena are performed. He was able, using energies from others, to move physical objects about and demonstrate seemingly miraculous manifestations. He believes, therefore that what we know as poltergeist phenomena are similar manifestations by etheric entities who employ the energies of some person present who either permits it or is so overflowing with energy (animal spirits) that its theft is not even noticed. Since these performances are largely mischievous and childish, he suspects they are the result of activity by discarnate childish spirits, who usually use the energies of living children who are present.

This lowering of the vibratory rate is extremely difficult to control and requires very sensitive handling. When the rate of the etheric body lowers beyond a certain point it automatically snaps back into the physical vehicle. Most experimenters are never successful in achieving any significant lowering of the etheric rate. However, many have reported raising it to almost sublime heights. They report that the atmosphere (so to speak) of the psychic world becomes finer and rarer as we free ourselves of sensual interests and satisfactions. The discomfort experienced in the physical state does not exist and as one ascends the feeling of well-being increases until it becomes a positive joyfulness.

One of the basic adjustments you have to make almost at the very beginning of your experience in the etheric state concerns the difference from the physical in moving from place to place. When you first free yourself from the physical body and are merely moving about your own bedroom or other rooms in your house or apartment, there is little difference. You walk about as before. But when you decide to go to a distant spot the procedure is different. Until you have learned the technique of mentally placing yourself where you wish to be—and this requires practice—the simplest way to go is by air—literally. To walk to most places takes too long, so you must learn to move yourself through the air somewhat in the manner of flying.

One experimenter in France described his experiences as follows:

> Since I knew nothing of the techniques used by birds, I hesitated to commit myself to the air. However, I knew how to swim, so telling myself that this etheric atmosphere is not too different from water, I threw myself into a horizontal position and went through the motions of swimming. To my amazement it worked. I found myself moving along about four feet above the ground at about the pace of a rapid walk and in that manner soon arrived at my destination.

Later on he reported further:

> I soon became quite proficient in this swimming technique and as I became more accustomed to the etheric medium in

which I moved, I learned more about its possibilities. Soon I assumed the position of diving, with my hands clasped and extending in front of me and my feet stretched out behind. In this horizontal position I found I could propel myself by merely wishing to move forward and that I could also regulate this speed from quite slow to exceedingly fast. Once, when moving at a great rate of speed, I decided on a whim to go straight up. In a second or two I found myself far above the earth, which looked small beneath me. Around me was the immense void of space. The experience was startling and breathtaking and I became so frightened that I returned instantaneously to my physical body with what I can only describe as a crash-landing. It hurt.

Thus, you see that while you may be ignorant of this new state when you first succeed in projecting from the body, you will gain confidence as you practice. The more you practice the more rapidly will you acquire skill, and gradually you will be able to separate the real from the illusory in all you encounter. Soon you will be sure enough of yourself to go back to mental projection, which will then take on an entirely new dimension. But this will only become real and understandable to you as you come to it. Right now a successful mental projection requires the use of only a small portion of your mind. Eventually, as your ability to use your mind expands, much vaster possibilities in mental projection will present themselves. True bi-location, the ability to move and act in two places at once, becomes possible, as do other seemingly miraculous powers. To you now, these may seem like the faculties of a god-like being beyond the reach of a mere mortal like yourself. But let me assure you there are many people walking the earth today who are capable of using these powers, people who do not look any different from you and who, when they started this work, had no more ability than you have at present. Through study and persevering practice they have developed their inherent capacities so that today they are almost god-like from the average man's viewpoint.

You, my friend, can do what they have done. What better time to start than now?

FOURTEEN

The Rosicrucian
Way of Life

Every man, woman and child in the world is advancing and developing, whether he or she realizes it or not. For some the rate of progress is slow; others go along at an average pace, a few are far out ahead. Each person is different. There are no carbon copies. Some strive to improve and others care for nothing but their own physical satisfactions. Those who want to develop and really try soon outdistance their fellows and come earlier to a true understanding of life. Their open minds, their intellectual curiosity and their persistent efforts bring them eventually to a Teacher who can lead them on the path to illumination and Cosmic Consciousness.

No one is contacted by such a Teacher until he has trained himself and is ready for the disciplines involved. You have often heard, "When the student is ready, the Master will appear." The important word in this promise is "ready." No one is ready by accident or by gift of Divine Providence. You get ready by training yourself, by study, by practicing certain exercises and by becoming skilled in the prescribed mental techniques. Along with this must go better understanding of who and what you are and why you do the things you do. All this, plus discipline and self-control, is part of the process of "getting ready."

Whether you are aware of it or not, you have actually started to get ready. The very fact that you have this book in your hand and are reading these words is proof of it True, your purpose in seeking it out may have been quite selfish, but there is no wrong in this. You may want more money, a better job, a new environment, a home, marriage, any number of worldly things. It makes very little difference what recognizable impulse caused you to dig into this book. The important fact is you *are* reading it and will benefit thereby. You can get the material things you want and you probably will. But you will also move at least a step or two up the ladder of your personal evolution and it is possible you may go much higher.

This book is largely a condensation of the teachings of the Rosicrucian Order, AMORC (an abbreviation for the Ancient Mystical Order Rosae Crucis), and is almost stenographic in its brevity. The chief reason for the existence of the Rosicrucian Order is to train you and others like you to the degree where you will be ready for the teaching of a Master. All the great world religions and all of the mystical and esoteric teaching organizations, and there are a great many, are dedicated to this same high purpose. But it is sadly true that only a few can truly inform a petitioner and completely train him to achieve this high object. Yet all do some good. As the Master Morya once said, "Even the smallest bonfire in the desert will attract a few stragglers."

But your purpose is not to just warm your hands. You want to know and you want to learn how to do. There are only a handful of esoteric schools in the world that can give you this training and the Rosicrucian Order, AMORC, is one of them, probably the best. For many years the general public held the belief that the Rosicrucian Order was started in Germany in the Seventeenth Century by a man named Christian Rosenkreutz from whom it got its name. But research in the present century has revealed that "Christian Rosenkreutz" was a symbolic name adopted by the current head of the Rosicrucians, and meant only a Christian of the Rosy Cross. Many documents have come to light with dates of Rosicrucian activities as early as the Twelfth and Thirteenth Centuries. The Encyclopaedia Britannica states that Cornelius Agrippa refers to the foundation of a branch in 1507 in which a "Brother Philalathes was invested with the power of Imperator" The Britannica further lists a book by "Omnis Moriar" which tells of a Rosicrucian Lodge in Germany in 1115 and lists also another in 1230 and Arnold de Villanova as an officer of the Order. There are numerous other dates given in records which are in libraries and collections available to the public. The private records of the Rosicrucian Order indicate it is much older and actually place the date of its origin back in the time of the Egyptian mystery schools and the reign of Thutmose III.

The most important quality of the Rosicrucian Order and one that sets it apart from other esoteric schools and fraternities is that it is not the teaching of one man. Over the years some of the world's greatest minds have contributed the results of their studies and experiments to the Order and the lessons today are a composite of the best offerings of these many minds. They are constantly being added to and revised in order to take advantage of the expanding consciousness of the average man. Truth does not change but today the general knowledge of electricity and other scientific advancements enables us to comprehend a great deal more than was possible to communicate even as recently as one hundred years ago.

Many well known and famous people have been Rosicrucians. Probably the most illustrious was the Pharoah Amenhotep IV, who was responsible for the creation of the original form of the Rosicrucian Order. Francis Bacon was Imperator of the Rosicrucian Order in the Seventeenth Century and Michael Maier was the Grand Master for Germany under his jurisdiction. Lord Raymund VI, Count of Toulouse, was a well-known Rosicrucian martyr in the days when it was dangerous to admit to any convictions other than those of the orthodox faith, and in more recent times M. F. Jollivet Castelot, the French chemist, was a Rosicrucian.

The Rosicrucian Order, AMORC, recognizes that every person has all sorts of ideas and convictions about himself and the world around him that bear no relation to the actual facts. An attempt is made with each new student to help him clear away some of these illusions. The hardest person to see and understand is yourself. Self-deception is the most common of all deceptions, and most of us grow old fondly believing that we are good and lovable creatures and the rest of the world is wrong. It is not easy to break through these walls of self-approval people build about themselves but if you are ever to realize even to a small degree on the great potential you possess, a certain clarity of vision and understanding is essential.

Thus I urge you for your own best interest to act on the suggestions given in this book. Don't take things for granted. Avoid inertia. Use your mind to appraise and evaluate the information offered. Apply your energy to the practice of the exercises recommended. Who knows? You may have the capacity to become another Francis Bacon, another John Dalton.

Let me tell you about John Dalton. It will illustrate how the Rosicrucian experimenters in the physical sciences inject certain advanced ideas into the mass consciousness of the scientific world. After acceptance and rejection by the leading scientists of the day and much mulling over, after an incubation period so to speak, these new discoveries are usually finally crystallized in acceptable form by some other scientist and become thereafter a part of the laws and principles of his particular discipline. Albert Einstein's ideas of relativity, for example, were first postulated when he was a young man, but did not register as part of accepted scientific knowledge until thirty years later. This was remarkable in that recognition came within his lifetime. Usually it does not.

John Dalton was an English chemist and physicist born in Cumberland in 1766. His father was a Quaker, a member of the Society of Friends, and John as a young man benefited by his father's tolerance and intelligent outlook. He was introduced to the Rosicrucian Order by John Gough, a blind scientist of considerable ability who was an officer in the Rosicrucian Fraternity. In the years between 1793 and 1815, Dalton made many discoveries, most of which he made public. He was the first to study and account for color blindness, his papers on the absorption of gases by liquids opened up whole new vistas for the world of manufacturing chemistry, but he is probably best known as the father of the Atomic Theory. After his death in 1844 his work was patronizingly referred to as "crude" by chemists and physicists in the latter part of the Nineteenth Century and the first quarter of the Twentieth. There is no pride quite so vain as intellectual pride, unfortunately. Since the mid-1940s, it has become clear that Dalton's ideas on the constitution of matter were far more accurate than the accepted standards prior to them. Today's understanding that the nucleus of the atom, once considered the basic minutia of mass, is made up of many finer particles was forecast by John Dalton over 150 years ago.

One of the basic Rosicrucian tenets is that all manifestation comes from energy and that for physical manifestation a triangle of energies is needed. It was Dalton's work with this Law of the Triangle that opened the door to his intuitive understanding of the subtlety of matter. However great his exposition of the Atomic Theory may be, an even greater contribution awaits understanding and interpretation. Between 1787 and the time of his death in 1844, Dalton kept a meteorological diary in which are recorded over 200,000 observations made by instruments constructed by himself. As early as 1793 he published an essay on these observations which contains the germs of his later conclusions. These have thus far been ignored by physicists and geophysicists and await only analysis and interpretation by some intuitively motivated modern Newton to open a whole new vista on the concept of motion.

The contents of this book comprise but a small fraction of the knowledge which the Rosicrucian Order disseminates freely to its members. A dozen such books could not contain it all. The information and instruction in each chapter barely skim the surface of the subject, which is treated in depth in the monographs. For example, in Chapter Seven, where healing is discussed, the visualization of color is not mentioned, because to treat with it thoroughly would take two or three chapters. For example if the individual you are treating is facing emotional problems and this is the cause of his ailment, then a pink or violet-pink color should be visualized as surrounding him. But if the ailment stems from a rundown physical condition, visualize a bright orange color in his aura.

Examining another area of interest, you might note the study of atmospheric conditions on human action. Even casual observation discloses how electric waves disturb the usual order. How much more profound must be the influence of the magnetic gales which occasionally sweep the planet. Another profitable study is the effect of motion on the human aura. We are urged to move rhythmically and avoid abrupt changes. Travelers complain of exhaustion after flying long distances by air. Is there a connection? Thus a whole new world waits to be explained. Is this not a challenge?

We learn by doing—so waste no time. If you would discover your hidden abilities and put them to work, start now. Thoughtful experiment and persistent striving are the keys. You must *do*. The techniques have been given. Your rate of progress is now up to you.